# PROCEEDINGS

*of the*

## ASSOCIATION OF ORTHODOX JEWISH SCIENTISTS

V

# Proceedings of the Associations

## of

# ORTHODOX JEWISH SCIENTISTS

Edited by
FRED ROSNER M.D.

**VOLUME 5**

**FELDHEIM PUBLISHERS**
Jerusalem • New York
5739 / 1979

ISBN 0-87306-150-0

Published by
*Feldheim Publishers*
*Jerusalem / New York*
for the
Association of Orthodox Jewish Scientists

*Printed in Israel*

# CONTENTS

# PREFACE

The appearance of Volume 5 of the *Proceedings of the AOJS* is another milestone in the histoiy of the Association. The enormous response to the request for manuscripts resulted in the submission of a large number of excellent papers, some of which, after appropriate revisions and editing, comprise the present work. Because of space limitations, several outstanding papers which were accepted for publication are being held over for Volume 6 of *Proceedings*, which we hope to publish within a year.

The opinions expressed in the various articles are solely those of the authors and do not necessarily represent the views of the Editorial Board of the *Proceedings* or of the AOJS.

I wish to express may gratitude to the Editorial Board (Yashar Hirshaut M.D., Rabbi Paul Kahn Ph.D., Rabbi Hugo Mandelbaum Ph.D., Rabbi Azriel Rosenfeld Ph.D., and Nora Smith M.D.) for reviewing the manuscripts. I also appreciate the advice of several consultants (Rabbi J. David Bleich Ph.D. and Professors Jacob Dienstag, Leo Levi and G.N. Schlesinger).

The officers and Executive Committee of the AOJS were helpful in aiding the final administrative stages of the publication of this volume and for that I am grateful. Finally, I am indebted to Mrs. Sophie Falk and Mrs. Miriam Regenworm for secretarial assistance.

FRED ROSNER, M.D.
*New York City*

# FOREWORD

With the issuance of Volume 5, *Proceedings* continues the tradition of publishing scholarly articles of excellence on the various ways Judaism and science interact. The high caliber of the papers is a testimony to the outstanding professional ability, coupled with deep Jewish learning, that characterizes the authors, most of whom are members of one of the AOJS organizations in the several countries. By the favorable reception accorded the previous volumes of *Proceedings*, the Jewish community has shown the interest and value it attaches to the pursuit of scientific studies within the encompassing and unifying framework of Orthodox Judaism. The Association of Orthodox Jewish Scientists in America is proud of the role it has had in the publication of this and other volumes of *Proceedings*, and looks forward to the issuance in the near future, אי״ה, of continuing volumes in the same series. Our thanks go to the Editor, Dr. Fred Rosner, and his Editorial Board for their indefatigable labors in bringing this volume to publication, and to the authors for their splendid contributions.

HERBERT GOLDSTEIN
*President, AOJS*

NORA SMITH
*Chairman of the Board, AOJS*

# TAY-SACHS DISEASE AND THE JEWISH COMMUNITY

## IMMANUEL JAKOBOVITS

Tay-Sachs is a rare congenital infants' disease of the brain and nerve cells, invariably leading to death at between 3 and 4 years of age following a long and painful process of degeneration. It occurs only in children whose parents are both latent cariers of it.

Tests in America, Britain and elsewhere have shown that carriers are ten times more common among Ashkenazi Jews than among other Jews or Gentiles — one in thirty Ashkenazi Jews as against one in three hundred others. When both parents are carriers the risk of their child being afflicted is one in four. That means the chance of a Jewish Ashkenazi Tay-Sachs child being born is one in 3,600 ($30 \times 30 \times 4$); among others it is one in 360,000 ($300 \times 300 \times 4$). In absolute terms, in a recent year out of nine cases in this country three were Jewish, whilst in America (where the proportion of Jews in the population is about four times as high as in Britain) it has been estimated (1971) that 70% of the 52 such patients born annually are Jewish.

In the absence of any known cure, and in view of the Jewish proclivity to the disease, the British Tay-Sachs Foundation proposed in 1972 carrying out a massive screening project among the Jewish community, aimed at examining 10,000 Jews a year (by a blood test) to ascertain whether they are carriers and, if so, to determine by a further amniotic fluid test during the 14th to

---

*Rabbi Dr. Immanuel Jakobovits is the Chief Rabbi of the British Commonwealth. For many years, Rabbi Jakobovits served as the spiritual leader of the "Fifth Avenue Synagogue" and the Rabbinic consultant of the AOJS. He authored the classic text* Jewish Medical Ethics *as well as several other books and numerous articles in the scientific and Jewish literatures, mostly dealing with Jewish medical ethics, a subject concerning which he is a recognized authority.*

*We are indeed privileged to publish Rabbi Jakobovits' article entitled "Tay-Sachs Disease and the Jewish Community". This article was originally published in 1976 in L'Eylah, a magazine issued by the Chief Rabbi's office for distribution among rabbis, communal leaders and other interested readers.*

16th week of any pregnancy whether it will produce a diseased child, with a view to the termination of such a pregnancy.

A screening operation on such a scale would require the active co-operation of synagogues and other Jewish organizations. To this end, the Foundation turned to the Board of Deputies and to me. Upon consultations with other ecclesiastical authorities, the Board was advised on 24th August, 1972 as follows:

> 1.   According to Jewish Law there is no objection to these tests being carried out within the Jewish community as proposed by the British Tay-Sachs Foundation and to synagogues and other Jewish communal agencies giving whatever assistance they can in the carrying out of this program.
> 2.   We wonder whether such tests could include single persons, so as to help avoiding the marriage of two carriers of the disease and the resultant chance of children afflicted with the disease being conceived.
> 3.   No general ruling can be given on the termination of pregnancies in cases where the generation of a diseased child is suspected or established. All such cases would have to be submitted to individual Rabbinic decisions. But this reservation does not affect the agreement to carry out the program as proposed.

However, before endorsing and recommending a scheme of such dimensions as requested, I felt that, apart from purely religious and moral considerations, it would be essential to bear in mind some wider communal ramifications which required expert medical advice. I therefore wrote in identical terms to Lord Cohen of Birkenhead and Lord Rosenheim as follows:

> 27th October, 1972
> The British Tay-Sachs Foundation proposes to undertake a massive "Screening Project" among the Jewish community, having regard to the fact that the disease is disproportionately prevalent among Ashkenazi Jews. In an effort eventually to carry out the requisite blood-tests on some 80,000 Jewish young persons, it is intended to organize this project through the active help of synagogues, Jewish clubs, etc. The Foundation has therefore approached me, as well as the Board of Deputies, to secure the endorsement of the community and the help of Jewish communal agencies through our sanction and encouragment of the proposed enterprise.

From the Jewish religious and moral point of view, I see no reason to withhold my support. The only proviso I have made on religious grounds — and this has been accepted by the Foundation — is that we would much prefer the effort to be concentrated on young people before they marry, so as to discourage marriages between two carriers of the disease, rather than on young married couples, where the tests would be useful as a "preventive" measure to prevent the birth of a Tay-Sachs child only by recourse to abortion.

However, a further factor which should be carefully considered has now been brought to my attention by a medical friend. It might be feared that by subjecting an entire community to these blood-tests, not to mention the attendant publicity which is bound to focus public attention on the Jewish proclivity to the disease, one might induce a communal "neurosis" by creating a state of undue anxiety or notoriety, especially among the less sophisticated members of the community. I understand from the Medical Director of the Foundation that the current annual incidence of the actual disease is estimated at 9 children in the country at large, including 3 Jewish children.

In the light of these considerations, I would deeply appreciate your considered opinion on whether the medical indications to prevent the annual birth of 3 such children outweigh the more intangible social counter-indications to warrant mass-testing of a specific section of the population as proposed. I would not wish to commit myself and the Jewish community to the support of such a massive program without the endorsement of the community's two most eminent medical personalities. I make this approach to you with the agreement of the Chairman and the Medical Director of the Foundation.

(sgd.) I. Jakobovits

Lord Cohen replied as follows:

1st November, 1972

I do *not* consider the proposed screening project should be supported in the form it is presented.

As you write, the current annual incidence of the disease is estimated at 9 in the U.K. of whom 3 are Jewish; since the duration of life of a child with Tay-Sachs disease is less than 4 years, there can never be more than 12 Jewish cases at any one time. There is no known treatment for the disease so that (unlike phenylketonuria) no benefit to the child follows its detection. Amniocentesis is not reliable in its results, and the risks of abortion are not negligible.

Even if two heterozygotes marry, the chances of an affected child are only 1 in 4. Thus, the exercise would be, if the requisite blood tests were carried out on 80,000 young persons, of whom of course many might refuse to be tested, a very costly procedure involving a great deal of technical manpower, of which there is a very short supply, which could be put to more potentially fruitful projects. I agree with you that the risks of a "communal neurosis" are by no means remote.

May I add one or two further comments:

1.  The figures given for gene frequency (by which I think is meant heterozygotes or carriers) appear to me to be taken from New York figures. It would be of interest to know if these are confirmed for the U.K. I should think that to test 1,000 Ashkenazi Jews would be sufficient.

2.  Tay-Sachs disease is only one of a group of genetically-determined diseases in which the nerve cells contain abnormal amounts of fatty and other substances which ultimately destroy them. A great deal of fundamental research is being carried out on the enzyme deficiencies which are responsible for these conditions. By a curious coincidence, I note in today's "Guardian" a reference to work at Keele University; and the Children's Research Fund, of which I am President, and Chairman of the Council, is supporting similar studies.

I have no objection to you showing this letter to the Chairman of the Foundation, for although the screening project is one which on a cost-benefit basis (apart from the other matter you raise) I could not conscientiously support, I would wholeheartedly urge support for more research into the fundamental mechanisms of this group of genetically-determined metabolic brain disorders.

(sgd.) Cohen of Birkenhead

From Lord Rosenheim the following two letters were received shortly before his death:

5th November, 1972

Thank you for your interesting letter. You ask a series of difficult and penetrating questions.

I have been able to talk about the matter with Professor Harry Harris, who is the Galton Professor of Genetics at University College, London, and Director of the Medical Research Council Unit on Human Bio-chemical Genetics. He told me that a Tay-Sachs Foundation was already active in the United States, but pointed out that people are more socially and ethnically conscious in the States than they are here. There is certainly a considerable risk of provoking anxiety in positive hetero-zygotes and the possibility of arousing some racial feeling.

On the other hand this condition, in which potential carriers can be detected and in which study of the amniotic fluid early in pregnancy can diagnose an affected infant, is clearly one of the conditions that lends itself best to this form of screening.

As I understood Professor Harris, he calculated that 1 in 3,600 Ashkenazi children might be born with the condition, and I imagine that this is in line with the observed numbers that you wrote to me about. This really raises the question of "Cost-Benefit" with the cost in terms of anxiety rather than hard cash.

(sgd.) Rosenheim

17th November, 1972

Further to my letter of November 5th, I have now had a talk with Dr. Philip Evans and have also discussed the screening problem with a group of doctors specially interested in screening.

I was impressed by Philip Evans and by the care with which the scheme for screening has been prepared, and I was interested to learn that a pilot trial of the scheme was being started in Wembley.

I am still doubtful about the "cost-benefit" in terms of anxiety and stress, but do appreciate that this is a serious attempt to get rid of a disease that itself causes great distress. I believe that it would be wise to wait for the results of the Wembley trial and would suggest that you should be able to get valuable impressions from the Rabbi and others concerned with encouraging young people to have the test.

I am sorry not to be more helpful. I think that you will note that I am scientifically in favour, but that humanity prompts caution.

(sgd.) Rosenheim

Following these exchanges, a number of pilot schemes were operated at several London synagogues and at Hillel House for students. Despite extensive publicity, including a full-page feature in the "Jewish Chronicle" and letters circulated among 7,000 general practitioners as well as among thousands of synagogue members, the results proved disappointing. Two years' efforts secured only a total of 341 volunteers, of whom 181 were unmarried. Altogether 16 were found to be carriers (1 in 21), and none of the couples tested were at risk.

Further screening projects were abandoned, as the Foundation came to the conclusion that the monitoring of pregnancies in women who already had Tay-Sachs babies was more rewarding. This was done in 20 cases of the infantile type of GM2 gangliosidosis, with 4 positive diagnoses, 4 terminations and 4 diagnoses confirmed. It was found that "at present in Britain, follow-up of families offers more than mass-screening does". (I am grateful to Dr. Philip Evans, the former Medical Director of the Foundation, for this information.)

---

Since then a great deal of communal screening has been carried out, with varying degrees of success, in several Jewish communities, notably in America, Israel and, for a short time, South Africa. Numerous medical papers have been published on the subject, as have a number of rabbinical responsa and statements. Some of this sizeable literature has quite recently been listed in a comprehensive survey by Dr. Fred Rosner, himself a senior hematologist and currently publication head of the American Association of Orthodox Jewish Scientists ("Tay-Sachs Disease: To Screen or Not to Screen", in *Tradition*, Spring 1976, pp. 101–112).

On the Jewish religious attitude, Dr. Rosner cites the views of Rabbi Moshe Feinstein (in an unpublished responsum of 1973)* and Rabbi J. David Bleich (*Or Ha-Mizrach*, Summer 1973, pp. 216 ff.; and *Tradition*, Winter 1972, pp. 145–148), as well as a statement by the Association of Orthodox Scientists (1973). While they encourage tests before marriage (only Rabbi Bleich prefers childhood or early adolescence; the others by contrast seek to avoid the nervous tension and prolonged anxiety which might result from testing young people not yet contemplating marriage), they all object to amniocentesis and to abortion if the test shows that the foetus is defective.

Dr. Rosner and his Association endorse this prohibition as absolute. But

---

* Now published in the *Rabbi Yechezkel Abramsky Memorial Volume*, Jerusalem, 5738.

they are evidently unaware of the more permissive verdicts given by other rabbis. Several leading authorities generally sanction the termination of a pregnancy with a high risk of an abnormal birth, e.g., through German measles, provided the abortion is performed within the first forty days, or in special cases even within the first three months (J. Weinberg, *Seridei Esh,* 3:17; S. Israeli, *Amud Hayemini,* 35; E. Waldenberg, *Tzitz Eliezer,* 9:51; see *No'am* 9:193–213, and 16, *Kunteres Harefu'ah,* 27). Dayan L. Grossnass of the London *Beth Din,* too, is inclined to permit an abortion if Tay-Sachs is confirmed, since such a child would in any event not be viable (*Lev Aryeh,* 2:205; see also my *Jewish Medical Ethics,* 1975, pp. 262–263 and 274–275).

# A COMPUTERIZED RETRIEVAL SYSTEM FOR THE RESPONSA LITERATURE — REVISITED

Yaakov Choueka, Menachem Slae
and
Samuel W. Spero

## 1. Introduction

In the lead article of volume 2 of these *Proceedings* — "A Retrieval System for the Responsa" — the author, Professor Aviezri S. Fraenkel, gave a comprehensive description of the Responsa Project, which had been initiated in 1967 with the express purpose of developing a computerized information retrieval system for the Responsa literature.

In this article, we propose to reintroduce the readers of these *Proceedings* to the Responsa Project. Rather than describing the Project from a technical point of view, however, we will be describing it here as to an audience of potential users.

---

*This paper is an adaptation of a larger work*: Y. Choueka, The Responsa Project, a Status Report, *Technical Report # 11, IRCOL, Bar-Ilan University (Ramat-Gan), June 1976, available upon request. Dr. Yaakov Choueka is a member of the Department of Mathematics and Computer Science at Bar-Ilan University. Rabbi Menachem Slae is a member of the Institute for Informational Retrieval and Computational Linguistics (IRCOL) at Bar-Ilan University. Dr. Samuel W. Spero is Professor of Mathematics at Cuyahoga Community College in Cleveland, Ohio and Education Specialist for IRCOL.*

*The Responsa Project was developed initially at the Weizmann Institute of Science (Rehovot) and Bar-Ilan University (Ramat-Gan) with the partial participation of the Institute for Research in Jewish Law, The Hebrew University (Jerusalem); it is now located at IRCOL at Bar-Ilan University, primarily supported by the National Endowments for the Humanities Fund (USA). Various phases and parts of the Project were also supported by the National Bureau of Standards (USA), the National Council for Research and Development (Israel), the National Academy of Sciences and Humanities (Israel), I.B.M. (Israel), and the Research Fund of the Israel Association of Insurance Companies.*

*The Retrieval System is being adapted for use in the United States.*

The general problem of locating material relevant to a given research topic and extracting it from a large corpus of data is, of course, not specific to the Responsa literature (although it is particularly acute there). Among the traditional tools created for solving these problems, familiar even to the general reader, are the card catalogue, the index printed at the end of a given book, or the various indexing journals commercially available for various fields of interest, e.g. *The Reader's Guide to Periodical Literature, Index Medicus, Business Index*, etc. Eventually, however, it was realized that such manual tools are no longer appropriate for modern information needs, for reasons having to do, partially at least, with the now famous (or perhaps infamous) "information explosion." The appearance of computers some two decades ago changed the scene in this area, as it did in so many other subjects. Two different approachs were developed for applying computers to the retrieval problem.

The first, more traditional one, was based on the idea of representing the document by some index, keyword, title, or some similar relevant "representative" (the indexing or abstracting being done either manually, or — more rarely — automatically) and programing the computer to retrieve those documents whose preassigned attributes correspond to the query specified by the user.

Many research topics are, however, complex in scope and highly specialized in nature, rendering the process of accurately and adequately indexing the textual material difficult, unsystematic and onerous, especially in those areas where it is difficult to foresee the user's needs and requests.

---

*Professor Aaron Schreiber, Principal Investigator for the N.E.H. grants, and Professor Aviezri Fraenkel, the initiator and leader of the Project for more than seven years, provided wise guidance and fruitful involvement.*

*All lists appearing in appendixes II, III, IV are as of June 1976 and were compiled by Z. Ilani, I. Pechenick and M. Slae.\**

*Reprints of many of the articles included in appendix III, and further information on the Project and on conducting searches on this database, may be obtained by writing to either of the first two authors at the Responsa Project (Bar-Ilan University, Ramat-Gan), or in the United States, to Professor A. Schreiber, School of Law, Temple University, Philadelphia.*

\* Note, however, that as of printing, Fall 1978, the operational database is composed of 128 volumes, including 29,700 responsa, 27,000,000 words, and that over 800 searches have been run. A detailed description is available upon request.

Thus, another line of approach was developed in which the whole text of the documents is inputted into the computer, and appropriate tools are supplied to the user for framing his query in the form of keyword combinations, citations and references which he thinks are apt to retrieve the relevant material. It was this approach that was adopted for the Responsa literature.

## 2. The Responsa Project

The Responsa Project was established to create a computerized information retrieval system for the *She'elot Uteshuvot*, based upon the full-text approach, enabling the same system to serve not only the *Talmid Chacham* and the jurist, but also the historian, the sociologist, the linguist, the educator and, in fact, any scholar interested in this literature, in retrieving relevant material from it.

It was for several very good reasons that out of all the various genres of Halachic literature, the Responsa literature was chosen for computerization.

First, it is the most difficult field of material for data location and document retrieval among the various fields of Halachic sources. For the majority of *Sifrut Chazal*, the famous Kossovsky Concordances are available or in preparation. From the Talmud, by use of *Ein Mishpat, Ner Mitzvah* of Rabbi Joshua Boaz, one quickly arrives at the relevant passages in the *Rambam, Tur* and *Shulchan Aruch* codes. Note also that these codes are in fact subject-arranged, and in a certain sense, "self-indexed," so that locating the appropriate material in these books is more or less straightforward. Also, many of the Halachic books follow the order of the above codes or of the Talmud.

Secondly, the Responsa is of the most value to the broadest spectrum of users, as we outlined above and as can be ascertained by a mere glance in Appendix III (list of search topics run on the system).

Spanning fifteen centuries, originating in literally every part of the world, and containing more than a quarter of a million documents, the Responsa literature is truly an invaluable storehouse of information that depicts the sociological, economic and historical conditions of 1500 years of Jewish wandering.

Thirdly, the growing interest in this literature from a wide spectrum of researchers and research groups, both rabbinic and academic, and the importance of supplying the *Poskim* with an almost indispensable tool that can give them, quickly and efficiently, a list of precedents to the problem at hand, shows that our system answers a real need.

Since its initiation through the efforts of Prof. A.S. Fraenkel, in 1967, the Project's activities have been centered around three primary goals:

a)  Establishing and maintaining a computerized databank containing the most important books of the Responsa literature, and operating the complex information-retrieval system designed to open up this literature to potential users;
b)  Conducting research programs in various special topics in Judaica and the Humanities, using the computerized information-retrieval system;
c)  Conducting basic research in computerized information-retrieval systems and in computational linguistics using the Responsa literature as the information system on which this research is based.

Basically, the aim has been to build a working "real-life" retrieval system for the Responsa literature, with optimal distribution of tasks between man and machine, where the emphasis is on "in-depth" searches. At the same time the system is used as a model for conducting basic research in computer sciences. Thus, fruits of the research have to pass ultimately the test of proving themselves useful in the real life environment of the Responsa Retrieval Project.

Some of these activities are detailed below. Numbers in parenthesis refer to the list of publications given in Appendix IV of this report. As indicated at the outset of this article, the computerized information system has long been operational.

As of the Spring of 1976, the mechanized database included 74 books of Responsa comprising some 18,000 Responsa (about 14,000,000 words), written in Spain, Germany, Algeria, France, Austria, Poland, Israel, Italy, Russia, Galicia, Switzerland, Egypt, Hungary, Turkey, Lithuania, Syria, Czechoslovakia, Holland, Ireland and Greece over a period of more than 800 years. A list of those books of Responsa presently included in the retrieval system together with the others projected for inclusion in the near future is given in Appendix II of this article.

## 3.  The Mechanized Database and Retrieval System

Whenever a Responsa book has been selected for incorporation in the database, it undergoes a data conversion cycle consisting of a bibliographical review, pre-editing, key-punching, and proofreading, until the whole text of the book is stored in the computer without any prior manual indexing. As soon as a significant number of books have been stored, they are merged into an integrated database, various internal working files (such as the text file, the dictionary and the concordance) are generated, and the documents are then available for mechanized search. For conducting a search, a user frames his request in the form of classes of words, key-word combinations, phrases, references, citations, etc., relevant to the search topic, and subject to various operators, whose function is to group the keywords in the various combinations required for the search.

For example, were we interested in customs of reading the Torah in Vilna, we could conceivably ask for all the documents that contain an occurrence of the combination *Keriat HaTorah* ("reading the Torah"), together with an occurrence of "Vilna" in the same paragraph. Broadly speaking, the user can specify that some keyword combinations should occur in the document at a certain distance (or between certain distance limits) from other words or that they co-occur in the same sentence or paragraph, etc.

The keyword combinations can also be combined by conjunction ("condition A and condition B must be satisfied by the documents"), disjunction ("condition A" or "condition B"), or negation ("condition A but not B").

The computer now scans the whole of the database and locates those documents satisfying the user's requirements, the results being printed in a variety of formats to enable the user to rapidly audit the output and determine the more relevant and interesting material. For fuller details see publications (A1) to (A13), (A16), (A17), (A22) and (A27) in Appendix IV. In Appendix I, we have an actual halachic searchframe explained at length; two more examples are given in (B1) and (B2).

One more point should be noted: Because of the highly inflected nature of the Hebrew language, and the additional linguistic problems specific to the Responsa literature (variant spellings, extensive use of abbreviations and acronyms, strong intermixture of Hebrew and Aramaic, etc.), the linguistic component of the Responsa system is of primary importance. In particular, special algorithms had to be developed for automatically performing conjugations, inflections and declensions, in order to generate all the valid grammatical variants of any "dictionary entry" presented by the user. For the linguistic problems, see (A8) and (A19).

EVALUATION OF THE SYSTEM'S PERFORMANCE

Besides the pragmatic evaluation from user feedback, which perhaps is the ultimate in system evaluation, as soon as the first version of the mechanized retrieval system was released, a controlled test was performed to evaluate the validity of the basic approach as well as the actual performance of the system. About 100 queries carefully chosen and phrased by outside specialists were run on a reduced database of 5 books (2500 documents — 1,300,000 words). The same queries were given to an outside team of experts, who were asked to use all traditionally available tools (including the reading of the entire database) for retrieving the relevant documents. The results were analyzed in depth, and it was found that the mechanized system retrieved about 98% of the relevant material, while the control group working manually retrieved only about 78%. Only in very rare cases did the computer miss an appropriate document, while the same was not infrequent with the manual group.

## 4.   Research in Judaica and the Humanities

A few interesting search topics and areas of application will be now described, by way of illustration.

a)   *Yiddish* — The pre-Yiddish vernacular terms and texts found in the Responsa stemming from the Ashkenazi dialects of the 13th–15th centuries are often unintelligible to the modern student, sometimes bearing only faint resemblance at best to present-day Yiddish. Dr. Yosef Barel of Bar-Ilan University's Yiddish Studies Program has prepared a dictionary of these terms, translated into Hebrew, together with their etymologies. The terms were gathered using the computerized retrieval system. A work has been published* covering those Ashkenazi Responsa texts found in the present database of the Project. The aid given to the student in understanding those texts is invaluable. This program is to be continued.

b)   *Insurance* — The Israeli Association of Insurance Companies has funded a research project in the topic "The Law and History of Insurance in Halakha Sources." The topic was searched both by computer and manually for those texts not computerized. A wealth of historical material, not available to the general historian of insurance, including records of Jewish marine insurance practices dating from 12th century France (Provence), 14th century Spain (Majorca), 15th century Algiers, and 16th and 17th century Turkey —

---

* Y. Barel, *A Yiddish Dictionary for the Responsa of Gedolei Ashkenaz*, Bar-Ilan Univ., Ramat Gan, 1977, 93 pp.

important early sources unknown from the standard historical works — has been discovered.

Many basic legal decisions based upon Halacha have similarly been recovered. An interim report summarizing about half of the historical legal finds has been published. See (B14) and (B15). A monograph is in preparation, to be published in Hebrew and separately in English translation.

c)  *Citation index to the Talmud* — A program of producing a list of citations of given pages of the Talmud in the Responsa Literature has been inaugurated.

Basically all mention of a specific tractate in the Talmud (and all references to such a tractate) are extracted from the database and sorted by the tractate page numbers. In such a way, a student of this tractate can easily find out where a given point of some *sugyah* has been interpreted or applied in the Responsa literature.

Such an index for tractate *Ketubot* is described and given in (B18). Similar indexes have since been published for *Baba Kama, Baba Batra, Gittin, Kiddushin* and *Yevamoth* and are available commercially.

d)  *Tiyul* — The term *Tiyul* in modern Hebrew usage is used for hikes, tours and outings. The varied and interesting uses of this term in the Responsa literature, and other sources in the Halacha, were searched and a major article depicting the uses of the term in Halacha was published. See (B16).

e)  *Educational applications* — An experimental education program for high-school students, aiming at interweaving the learning of the Talmud with the study of appropriate Responsa literature, was recently started. Three workbooks, on tractates *Betzah, Baba Batra* and *Sukkah*, have already been issued and class-tested (B10), (B11) and (B17). In such a workbook, every studied topic (*sugyah*) of the corresponding tractate is enriched by appropriate Responsa that interpret it or demonstrate its application to real-life situations. These workbooks have been tested in Yeshiva high-school classes in Israel with positive feed back. The Ministry of Education is now funding a trial of these study aids.

A teacher's in-service training program for teachers of *Torah SheB' Al Peh* ("Oral Law") has been inaugurated. The purpose of this program is to train the teachers in the use of the computerized Responsa search and its applications for literature searching and in-depth research. A two-year program of courses was completed.

## 5. Research and Development Program (information retrieval and computational linguistics)

a)  *On-line retrieval for the Responsa literature* — Our main effort will be devoted in the near future to the completion of an on-line retrieval system for the mechanized Responsa database. The idea is to allow the user to have direct access to the database, via a video terminal, and to freely "browse" in it, using a convenient Conversational Language. Thus, the user will specify some keyword combinations, or any other condition, will get an immediate reply on the screen, will ask for the display of some relevant sentences or paragraphs, after which he will modify the search request, asking for a new display, now and then printing some relevant information, etc. It is believed that such an improvement will greatly enhance the System's usefulness and accessibility. As of Summer 1978 about half of the search program has been converted to an on-line mode.

b)  *KEDMA — Linguistic files in retrieval systems* — Because of the complex nature of Hebrew morphology, any automatic processing of Hebrew texts must contain a linguistic component for the mechanical grammatical analysis of a given Hebrew word (in particular: finding the word's corresponding "dictionary entry" and "root"). The aims of the KEDMA sub-project are to provide a flexible tool that can be incorporated in any automatic Hebrew text processing system (including the Responsa system) for solving these problems. Using grammatical algorithms as well as available dictionaries, a huge magnetic file (about 2.5 million records) containing an exhaustive thesaurus of all Hebrew words (without prepositions) has been produced. To every word in this file, lexical and morphological information is appended. A highly condensed version of this thesaurus, coupled with special algorithms for prepositions' analysis, will enable the producing of "local" files, tailored to the specific database, and these in turn will make possible an efficient and on-line processing of the information.

A second and corrected version of the thesaurus is under way, and this version will be used to build the local files of the Responsa database which will replace the "grammatical synthesis" component of the system, described in (A11) and (A19).

c)  *Mechanical resolution of lexical ambiguity* — Lexical ambiguity — due mainly to the omission of vowels and certain other diacritical marks in written Hebrew — is a very serious problem in the automatic processing of

Hebrew texts. A word can be assigned, on the average, four different "meanings" (dictionary entries), and in certain cases, even tens of meanings. The research is concerned with techniques for the automatic resolution of such ambiguities by the computer.

These techniques are ultimately to be incorporated as standard components in the System. See (A25).

d) *Automatic construction of Hebrew concordances with ramifications to English concordances* — The omission of vowels in printed Hebrew texts and the highly inflected nature of the language have the effect of scattering the grammatical variants of any word all over an alphabetical listing of a text. Similar problems exist in English (consider e.g.: go, went; goose, geese), but are less severe. A central problem of automatic concordance construction is to minimize the manual editing required for collecting these different variants.

The contribution made here towards solving this problem is to define *equivalence classes* of the appearances of any text-word, based upon the nature of the right and the left "text-neighbors" of these appearances. These classes permit classifying the appearances according to their semantic meanings. The method was tested on a database of half a million words, where it turned out that about half of the manual editing effort may be saved.

To illustrate, sorting of all occurrences of *Av* ("father"; "the month of Av") by the words immediately preceeding or succeeding these occurrences, will exhibit a certain number of patterns such as *Kibud Av* or *Tisha BeAv*, and will enable the automatic ascription of all the occurrences of the same pattern to the same class. See (A18).

e) *Iterative searches* — Rather than run a search one time with a full search strategy as at present, a second approach is conceivable: that of using a series of search runs, each run being based upon a modification of the previous one, the changes being suggested by a computerized automatic audit of the search returns, and a new key-word list submitted, based upon an analysis of the vocabularies of the relevant documents returned, as judged by the user. Thus, a primitive search is framed with only a few "strong" keyword phrases, the results returned are subjected to a statistical analysis, additional keyword phrases are suggested by the finds in the database, and a second run performed, the process repeated, a third search frame run, and so on, until a saturation po int is reached.

Several tests were conducted on a database of U.S. Patents. First exploratory experiments were also made with the Responsa database. Very consistently, the best results were obtained by using strictly local clustering with metrical constraints — a method which can be adapted to very large databases. See (A20).

## APPENDIX I *

### SAMPLE SEARCH

a) *Topic*: *Recovery of expenditures in breach of promise* — Is one who breaches a promise to marry liable for the expenditures made by the fiance(e) (*Hafarat Shidduchim*)?

Two distinct types of recoveries are considered: (i) *gifts* of property from one party to the other (*Matanot*); (ii) purely monetary *expenses* (*Hotza'ot*) incurred in the performance of those acts demanded by custom, such as festive meals, monetary gifts to servants, contributions to charity, and travel expenses for visiting. The legal question dealt with in the first category is usually ownership of the property (return of the gift), whereas the second, since it deals with repayment of funds laid out, is a part of the law of torts, more precisely, *indirect damage*, as the defendant committed no direct physical act of injury; indeed, the damage was committed by the injured party upon himself. In the relevant legal literature, as in real life, both problems are usually intertwined.

b) *Sources* — The primary source for the legal discussion of the expenses topic is a case found in the *Mishneh Torah Code* of the Rambam (Maimonides), where the groom-to-be made the customary party for his friends and distributed gifts, and the bride-to-be then broke the engagement. Rambam, following precedent, finds against the bride in such cases and requires repayment of all expenses. Ravad (Rabbi Abraham ben David, 12th century, Provence), Rambam's arch-critic, disagrees, basing himself upon a Talmudic decision wherein one who sells defective seed is liable only for the cost of the seed, but not for the expenses incurred by the buyer in unsuccessfully planting such seed. Thus we see — maintains Ravad — that if the immediate act of injury is performed by the plaintiff himself, but not by the original causer of the loss, the indirect act of damage involved cannot generate liability. The commentators to the Code explain Rambam's position as differentiating be-

---

* *Adapted from* Y. Choeuka, M. Cohen, J. Dueck, A. S. Fraenkel and M. Slae, "Full Text Document Retrieval: Hebrew Legal Texts," *Proc. ACM Symposium on Information Storage and Retrieval* (J. Minker and S. Rosenfeld, eds.), University of Maryland, April 1971, p. 74.

tween an act of business, such as the seed transaction, and an act dictated
by local custom, as in our case of engagement. In the latter, one is liable
even for what would normally be considered an indirect cause of damages.
The later codes side with Rambam, and such is the accepted practice in the
courts (see *Shulchan Aruch, Even HaEzer,* Section 50, paragraph 3, and
*Aruch HaShulchan, loc. cit.*).

c)   *General search strategy* — Following is a list of the keywords and key-
phrases to be used in the mechanized search.

| KEYWORD COMBINATIONS | EXPLANATIONS |
|---|---|
| 1. (Tractate) *Baba Batra* (Folio #) 92 | Talmudic source germane to our topic |
| 2. (vegetable) seeds (*Zaronim*) | Subject of discussion in the text of the above Talmudic citation |
| 3. Rambam, *Zechiah U'Matanah,* Chapter 6 | Reference to code dealing with the problem |
| 4. (Prevalent) custom (*Minhag*), feast (*Mishteh*), breach (*Hefer*), cause of damage (*Garam*) | Terms used by Rambam in #3 |
| 5. *Even HaEzer* (Sect.) 50 | Reference to later code |
| 6. (Marriage) agreement (*Shidduch*), gifts (*Matanot*), expenditures (*Hotza'ot*) | Other terms germane to the topic, taken from the literature |

d)   *Definition of search sets and operators* — The keyword terms below are
defined in the order of (c) above. Each term contains, in actuality, all grammatical variants of the given single entry which occur in the database.

Note that a document quoting a source frequently brings only the reference or the citation, not both. When we want to retrieve such a document,
we thus designate it as relevant if it contains either the reference or the
citation.

1.   The keywords *Baba* and *Batra,* one word apart (*Baba Batra*), and the
folio #"92" in the same sentence ("B. B. 92").

2.   The keywords "Rambam", "Zechiah U'Matanah" (appearing one word
apart) and "Chapter 6" appearing in the same paragraph.

3.   3/5 of the terms "custom", "feast", "breach", "agreement" and "gifts"
appear in the same document.

4. The key words "Even" and "HaEzer" one word apart, and "50" appearing in the same sentence.

5. "Marriage agreement" and "Expenditure" appearing in the same document.

6. "Seeds" and "indirect cause (of damage)" appearing in the same document.

# APPENDIX II

## I. Responsa Collections Forming Operative Database

Legend: R. = Rabbi; b. = *ben* (son of); p.o. = photo offset edition.

Spellings of names, places and texts, as well as dates, are taken from the *Encyclopedia Judaica* whenever possible. Further bio-bibliographical details are usually available in the base article of the *Judaica*. Note however that we have used "ch" in place of the "ḥ" used in the *Judaica* spellings, and "tz" for "z" or "ẓ".

Certain texts computerized by the Project were enhanced with text corrections from previous editions. These are so labelled in this table. These text corrections are clearly marked as such in the computer edition, and are usually pragmatic, rather than systematic or comprehensive.

| TEXT: RESPONSA OF | AUTHOR | EDITION | NO. RESPONSA | NO. WORDS (IN THOUSANDS) |
|---|---|---|---|---|
| **A. Spain, Rishonim (until 16th century)** | | | | |
| 1. Rabad (Ravad) | R. Abraham b. David, c. 1125–1198, Posquieres, Provence | Kafich, Mosad HaRav Kook, Jerusalem, 1964 | 232 | 131 |
| 2. Ramban (Nachmanides) | R. Moses b. Nachman, 1194–1270, Spain | Assaf, Jerusalem, 1967; p.o. Mekitzei Nirdamim, 1935 | 87 | 28 |
| 3. Rashba*, Part I | R. Solomon b. Abraham Adret, c. 1235–1310, Barcelona, Spain | Bnei Brak, Israel, 1958 | 1252 | 361 |
| 4. " " II | " | " (some corrections added from Leghorn edition, 1657) | 400 | 184 |

* Comments and text corrections were added to entire set from *Collected Responsa of Rashba*, R.E.S. Wasserman, appended to *Kovetz He'arot, Yebamot*, R.E. Wasserman.

| TEXT: RESPONSA OF | AUTHOR | EDITION | NO. RESPONSA | NO. WORDS (IN THOUSANDS) |
|---|---|---|---|---|
| 5. Rashba, Part III | R. Solomon b. Abraham Adret | Bnei Brak, 1965 | 446 | 167 |
| 6. " " IV | " | Jerusalem, 1960; p.o. St. Petersburg, 1883 | 327 | 110 |
| 7. " " V | " | Jerusalem, 1960; p.o. Vilna, 1885 | 293 | 104 |
| 8. " " VI** | " | Jerusalem, 1960; p.o. Warsaw, 1868 | 286 | 28 |
| 9. " " VII** | " | " " | 539 | 47 |
| 10. Rashba, attributed to Ramban (arbitrarily called VIII in Project use) | " | Jerusalem, 1970; p.o. Warsaw, 1884 | 288 | 128 |
| 11. Rosh | R. Asher b. Jechiel, c. 1250–1327, Germany, Spain | New York, 1954; p.o. Vilna, 1885 | 965 | 325 |
| 12. Ritba (Ritva) | R. Yom Tov b. Abraham Ishbili (Asbili), c. 1250–1330, Spain | Kafich, Mosad HaRav Kook, Jerusalem, 1959 | 209 | 127 |
| 13. Zichron Yehudah | R. Judah b. Asher (Rosh), 1270–1349, Germany, Spain | Jerusalem, 1965; p.o. Berlin, 1846 | 101 | 72 |
| 14. Chazei HaTenufah | R. Moses de Brussels, 14th century, Spain | Appended to the *Chayim Sha'al* responsa collection, N.Y., 1961; p.o. Lemberg, 1886 | 64 | 6 |
| 15. Ribash (Rivash) | R. Isaac b. Sheshet Perfet, 1326–1408, Spain, Algiers | New York, 1954; p.o. Vilna, 1879 | 518 | 560 |
| 16. Tashbetz, Part I | R. Simeon b. Tzemach Duran (Rashbatz), 1361–1444, Majorca-Algiers | Jerusalem, 1960; p.o. Lemberg, 1891 | 178 | 230 |

** Text corrections and comments added from *Responsa of Rashba Vol. VI*, edited by M. Luria, Jerusalem, 1903.

| TEXT: RESPONSA OF | AUTHOR | EDITION | NO. RESPONSA | NO. WORDS (IN THOUSANDS) |
|---|---|---|---|---|
| 17. Tashbetz, Part II | R. Simeon b. Tzemach Duran | Jerusalem, 1960; p.o. Lemberg, 1891 | 296 | 167 |
| 18.   ,,   ,, III | ,, | ,,      ,,      ,, | 327 | 166 |
| 19.   ,,   ,, IV | | ,,      ,,      ,, | 127 | 255 |
| *Chut HaMeshullash* | R. Solomon Duran, R. Solomon Tzror, R. Abraham Ibn Tawah; all 16th century, Algeria | | | |
| **B. Ashkenaz, Rishonim (France, Germany, Austria, Northern Italy, et al., until 16th century)** | | | | |
| 20. *Sefer HaYashar* (Responsa section) | R. Jacob b. Meir Tam (Rabbenu Tam), c. 1100–1171, France | Israel, 1965; p.o. Berlin, 1898 | 103 | 95 |
| 21. *Min HaShamayim* | R. Jacob of Marvege (Meirous), 12–13th century, France | Margoliot, Mosad HaRav Kook, Jerusalem, 1957 | 88 | 30 |
| 22. Maharam MiRothenberg Vol. IV | R. Meir b. Baruch of Rothenberg, c. 1215–1293, Germany | Tel Aviv, 1969; p.o. of Bloch edition, Budapest, 1895 | 1023 | 248 |
| 23. Maharach Or Zarua | R. Chayim (Eliezer) b. Isaac Or Zarua, 13th century, Austria, Germany (the father authored the famous *Or Zarua*) | Jerusalem, 1960; p.o. Leipzig, 1860 | 261 | 139 |
| 24. *Terumat HaDeshen*, Part I | R. Israel b. Petachyah Isserlein, 1390–1460, Austria, Germany | Israel, 1974; p.o. Warsaw, 1882 (text corrections and reference citations were inserted to the p.o. edition by the editors) | 354 | 172 |
| 25.   ,,      ,, Part II | ,, | ,,      ,,      ,, | 267 | 69 |
| 26. Mahari Weil | R. Jacob b. Judah Weil, d. before 1456, Germany | Jerusalem, 1959 | 193 | 85 |
| 27. *Sefer Leket Yosher*, Part I (*Orach Chayim*) | R. Joseph b. Moses, 1423–1490(?), Germany | Jerusalem, 1969; p.o. Berlin, 1903 | 571 | 82 |

| TEXT: RESPONSA OF | AUTHOR | EDITION | NO. RESPONSA | NO. WORDS (IN THOUSANDS) |
|---|---|---|---|---|
| 28. *Sefer Leket Yosher*, Part II (*Yoreh De'ah*) | R. Joseph b. Moses, 1423–1490(?), Germany | Jerusalem, 1969; p.o. Berlin, 1903 | 228 | 55 |
| 29. Maharik | R. Joseph b. Solomon Colon, c. 1420–1480, Italy | Jerusalem, 1973; p.o. Warsaw, 1884 (corrections and citation references inserted into p.o. edition by editors) | 192 | 333 |
| **C. 16th Century (period of Shulchan Aruch)** | | | | |
| 30. Maharam Alashkar | R. Moses b. Isaac Alashkar, 1466–1542, Spain, Greece, Egypt, Israel | Jerusalem, 1956 | 121 | 189 |
| 31. Mahari Berab | R. Jacob Berab, c. 1474–1541, Spain, Israel | Jerusalem, 1958 (corrections added from Venice, 1663 edition) | 62 | 114 |
| 32. Radbaz, Part I | R. David b. Solomon Ibn Avi Zimra, 1479–1573, Spain, Egypt, Israel | Jerusalem, 1972; p.o. Warsaw, 1882 | 842 | 373 |
| 33.     ,,    II | ,, | ,, | 235 | 172 |
| 34.     ,,    III | ,, | ,, | 292 | 197 |
| 35.     ,,    IV | ,, | ,, | 307 | 133 |
| 36.     ,,    V | ,, | ,, | 290 | 106 |
| 37.     ,,    VI | ,, | ,, | 73 | 54 |
| 38.     ,,    VII | ,, | ,, | | |
| 39. *Avkat Rochel* | R. Joseph b. Ephraim Caro, 1488–1575, Spain, Turkey, Israel | Jerusalem, 1960; p.o. Leipzig, 1859 | 217 | 289 |
| 40. Mahari Ben Lev (Maharival), Part I | R. Joseph b. David Ibn Lev, 1505–1580, Turkey | Jerusalem, 1960 | 126 | 183 |
| 41.     ,,    ,,    II | ,, | ,, | 89 | 133 |

| TEXT: RESPONSA OF | AUTHOR | EDITION | NO. RESPONSA | NO. WORDS (IN THOUSANDS) |
|---|---|---|---|---|
| 42. Rema | R. Moses b. Israel Isserles, 1525, 1530(?)–1572, Poland | Ziv edition, Jerusalem, 1971 | 133 | 327 |
| 43. Maharam Alshech | R. Moses Alshech, d. after 1593, Turkey, Israel | New York, 1961; p.o. Lemberg, 1789 | 140 | 256 |
| 44. Maharshal | R. Solomon b. Jechiel Luria, 1510(?)–1574, Poland | Jerusalem, 1969 | 101 | 133 |
| 45. Maharam Galante | R. Moses b. Mordechai Galante, 16th century, Italy, Israel | Jerusalem, 1960 | 125 | 115 |
| 46. Ranach | R. Eliyah b. Chayim, 1530(?)–1610(?), Turkey | Jerusalem, 1960 | 123 | 335 |
| 47. *Be'er Sheva* | R. Issacher Dov b. Israel Lazar Eilenburg, 1550–1623, Italy | Jerusalem, 1969; p.o. Warsaw, 1890 | 75 | 68 |
| 48. Maharam MiFano | R. Menachem Azariah da Fano, 1548–1620, Italy | Jerusalem, 1963 | 130 | 126 |
| 49. Bach, *Yeshanot* ("older edition") | R. Joel Sirkes, 1561–1640, Poland | New York, 1966; p.o. Ostrow, 1834 | 158 | 250 |
| 50. Bach, *Chadashot* ("new edition") | " | Jerusalem, 1959 | 106 | 173 |
| **D. 17th-19th Centuries** | | | | |
| 51. *Hilchot Ketanot* | R. Jacob Chagiz, 1620–1674, Israel | Cracow, 1897 | 571 | 77 |
| 52. *Chut HaMeshullash,* Part I | R. Chayim b. Isaac Volozhiner, 1749–1821, Russia | Israel, 1968; p.o. Vilna, 1882 | 28 | 84 |
| 53. " " II | R. Hillel of Volozhin, 19th century, Russia (son-in-law of R. Chaim, above) | " " " | 8 | 24 |

| TEXT: RESPONSA OF | AUTHOR | EDITION | NO. RESPONSA | NO. WORDS (IN THOUSANDS) |
|---|---|---|---|---|
| 54. *Chut HaMeshullash*, Part III | R. Eliezer Isaac Fried, 19th century, Russia (son-in-law of R. Isaac, the son of R. Chaim) | Israel, 1968; p.o. Vilna, 1882 | 61 | 99 |
| 55. Chatam Sofer, Part I (*Orach Chayim*) | R. Moses Sofer, 1762–1839, Germany, Hungary | Chatam Sofer Institute, Jerusalem, 1972 | 208 | 253 |
| 56. ,, ,, V (*Choshen Mishpat*) | ,, | New York, 1958; p.o. Pressburg, 1862 | 176 | 214 |
| 57. ,, ,, VII (collected responsa) | ,, | Chatam Sofer Institute, Jerusalem, 1972 | 73 | 100 |
| 58. *Yeshuot Malko* | R. Israel Joshua Trunk, 1820–1893, Poland | New York, 1958; p.o. St. Petersburg, 1927 | 281 | 132 |
| 59. *Be'er Yitzchak* | R. Isaac Elchanan Spektor, 1817–1896, Lithuania | New York, 1948; p.o. Koenigsburg, 1860 | 86 | 341 |
| 60. *Meshiv Davar* | R. Naphtali Tzvi Judah Berlin, 1817–1893, Lithuania | Jerusalem, 1968; p.o. Vilna, 1881 | 260 | 348 |
| 61. *She'ilat David* | R. David b. Samuel Friedmann ("Reb Davidel Karliner"), 1828–1917, Lithuania | New York, 1966; p.o. St. Petersburg, 1913 | 55 | 251 |
| 62. Maharsham, Part I | R. Shalom Mordechai Shvadron 1835–1911, Galicia (Poland) | New York, 1962; p.o. Warsaw, 1902 | 230 | 290 |
| 63. ,, ,, II | ,, | New York, 1962; p.o. St. Petersburg, 1905 | 270 | 337 |
| 64. ,, ,, III | ,, | New York, 1962; p.o. Satamar, 1910 | 377 | 354 |
| 65. ,, ,, IV | ,, | New York, 1962; p.o. Lemberg, 1913 | 151 | 187 |

| TEXT: RESPONSA OF | AUTHOR | EDITION | NO. RESPONSA | NO. WORDS (IN THOUSANDS) |
|---|---|---|---|---|
| 66. Maharsham, Part V | R. Shalom Mordechai Shvdron | New York, 1962; p.o. Satamar, 1926 | 84 | 180 |
| 67. *Melammed LeHo'il* | R. David Tzevi Hoffmann, 1843–1921, Hungary, Germany | New York, 1954; p.o. Frankfort A.M. 1926–1932 | 373 | 204 |
| **E. 20th Century** | | | | |
| 68. *Mishpat Cohen* | R. Abraham Isaac Kook, 1865–1935, Russia, Israel | Jerusalem, 1966 | 150 | 194 |
| 69. *Da'at Cohen* | " | " | 242 | 262 |
| 70. *Ezrat Cohen* | " | " | 109 | 214 |
| 71. *Seridei Esh*, Vol. III | R. Jechiel Jacob Weinberg, 1885–1966, Russia, Germany, Switzerland | Jerusalem, 1974 | 134 | 260 |
| 72. *Yabbia Omer*, Vol. I | R. Ovadia Yosef, born 1920, Israel, Egypt | Jerusalem, 1974 | 70 | 339 |
| 73.   "   "   IV | " | Jerusalem, 1964 | 108 | 488 |
| 74.   "   "   V | " | Jerusalem, 1969 | 100 | 423 |
| | | Total: | 18,165 | 13,882 |

Note: As of end of 1978, c. 128 texts are operational. List available from Responsa Project.

II.  Texts Converted to Computer Tape but Not Yet Merged with Operative Database

| TEXT: RESPONSA OF | AUTHOR | EDITION | NO. RESPONSA | NO. WORDS (IN THOUSANDS) |
|---|---|---|---|---|
| 1. *Chavot Ya'ir* | R. Jair Chayim b. Moses Samson Bacharach, 1638–1702, Germany | Lemberg, 1894 | 239 | 338 |
| 2. Noda Biyehudah, I | R. Ezekiel b. Judah Landau, 1713–1793, Poland, Prague | Jerusalem, 1969; p.o. Warsaw, 1880 | 277 | 596 |
| 3. " " II | " | " | 595 | 724 |
| 4. *Ein Yitzchak,* Part I | R. Isaac Elchanan Spektor, 1817–1896, Lithuania | New York, 1965; p.o. Vilna, 1889 | 147 | 499 |
| 5. " " II | " | New York, 1965; p.o. Vilna, 1895 | 70 | 292 |
| 6. R. Abraham b. HaRambam | R. Abraham b. Moses b. Maimon (= b. Maimonides), 1186–1237, Egypt | Freimann, Jerusalem, 1938 | 128 | 50 |
| 7. *Birkat Avraham* | " | Jerusalem, 1960; p.o. Lyszk, 1860 | 47 | 39 |
| 8. *Ma'aseh Nissim* | " | K. Cahana, appended to Mishne Torah, Tel-Aviv, 1957 | 13 | 32 |
| 9. Maharik *HaChadashot* (New series) | R. Joseph b. Solomon Colon, c. 1420–1480, Italy | Pines, Jerusalem, 1970 | 361 | 129 |
| 10. HaRe'em | R. Elijah Mizrachi, c. 1450–1526, Constantinople | Jerusalem, 1938 | 100 | 269 |
| 11. Maharashdam, Vol. I | R. Samuel b. Moses de Medina, 1506–1589, Salonika | New York, 1959; p.o. Lemberg, 1862 | 486 | 677 |
| 12. Maharashdam, Vol. II | R. Samuel b. Moses de Medina, 1506–1589, Salonika | New York, 1959; p.o. Lemberg, 1862 | 461 | 541 |

‏חו__שוטר לבית יצחק ולחנ ווחו.

‏ז:__שוטר, או פאירש.

‏יז__שוטר ומושל.
‏לא שוטר ולא מושל; אם חרצה לתח אוחו ברצוז, תחנהו. ואם לאו.
‏לא__שוטר ולא מושל. אם חרצה לתח אוחו ברצוז. תחנהו. ואם לאו.
‏ס._שוטר העיר, עד שהגיעו לגשר כפר פורקש.
‏ק.__שוטר. ומושל; לפטור ולהוציא עצמו מכלל ההודאות.

‏יז__שוטר המלד עומד עליו לומר דייניה לפלניא ואי לא עטילונ ‏לז

‏או__שוטר העיר בבית הכנסת ביום הנורא ריש שחא יגרמו שהשוטר דחף

‏או__שוטר או מושל לוקח משכון מישראל אז ודאי איז מקוהו לו
‏יז__שוטר ומושל את נדרה אלא שוחכי יכול להחירה ויש חולקי

‏יז__שוטר ומושל ודינה אינה רוצה להסתלק מתנוייה מתנוייה יורנו רר יו ‏*

‏לא__שוטר ולא מושל אלא הוא לגזו והוא זבר עמו עד שהרצ השטר

‏את__שוטר ומושל העיר ובהיותו שם ברומה לקחו כל אשר לו מבית

‏זור הערות המודפסות וספר.
‏שר השורה.                     ‎%=אחוז של הפסקה.

**Printout of K.W.I.C. format for search: "Poli** and Policemen". The key word, shoter, is print

| סימן | ד"ה | % | 4 -שו"ת הרשב"א חלק ב |
|---|---|---|---|
| — | --- | ----- | - ---- ------ ----- - |
| ג_____שאלת_יצ'_10%____ | | | |

| סימן | ד"ה | % | 4 -שו"ת הרשב"א חלק ג |
|---|---|---|---|
| — | --- | ----- | - --- ----- --- - |
| שפה____תשונה_מ'_60%____ | | | זעלמא, אלא: אנשים שיש להם רשות מצ |

| סימן | ד"ה | % | 9 -שו"ת הריב"ש |
|---|---|---|---|
| — | --- | ---- | ----- ---- --- - |
| עו_____תשונה_מ_2_90%____ | | | ושלש נשים, ואיז מכלים, שכד נהגו, ואא" |
| קכז | | שאלה מ ע' 70% | כי איז כאן כח, שאיז מי שיכר |
| ועתה_יש__10%____ | | | כי איז כאן כח ואיז מי שיכר |
| רסו____לדוז_של'_90%____ | | | ולא יכלו לצאה מז העיר, אם לא ש |
| תס_____עוד_שאלת_1%____ | | | שישתדל עם הגבירה, יר"ה, או עם |

| סימן | ד"ה | % | 10-שו"ת חשב"ץ חלק א |
|---|---|---|---|
| — | --- | ----- | - --- ---- ------- |
| קנח____עוד_יי_(1)_50%____ | | | אש יבך בזה ואומר שהדבר ידוע שהוא אינ |

| סימן | ד"ה | % | 16-שו"ת מהרי"י וויל |
|---|---|---|---|
| — | --- | ----- | ----- ---- ------- |
| קמ_____אצילי_א'_50%____ | | | הוה על הוה שמעתי איך שהאנשים ה |

| סימן | ד"ה | % | 19-שו"ת מהרי"ק |
|---|---|---|---|
| — | --- | ----- | ------ ----- - |
| טו_____אורד_ימ'_30%____ | | | הזה אלא אפיי למה שכתב בסמ"ק וז"ל |
| ג_____על_דנ_80%____ | | | נודרה אלא שעושה כנור אלמנה וגרושה |

| סימן | ד"ה | % | 25-שו"ת אבקת רוכל |
|---|---|---|---|
| — | --- | ---- | ---- ---- ------ |
| צג_____שאלה_רא'_60%____ | | | או כתובתז כפי צוואת אחיהם ולא |

| סימן | ד"ה | % | 27-שו"ת מהרשד"ם חלק יו"ד |
|---|---|---|---|
| — | --- | ----- | ---- --- ------- ---- |
| עז_____הקהל_ה_ו'_90%____ | | | וחתמו והחתימו נשבע שבועות נוראו |

| סימן | ד"ה | % | 27-שו"ת מהרשד"ם חלק חו"מ |
|---|---|---|---|
| — | --- | ----- | ---- --- ------- ------- |
| נד_____ילמדנו_30%____ | | | ברומה לעמוד על נפשו כי ראה כי כלתה |

ד"ה=דיבור המחחיל .

/=מדברי מתקין הספר מטעם ה
*=יש מילת מן

the middle of the line; the reference appears at
he right of the line-of-quote.

| TEXT: RESPONSA OF | AUTHOR | EDITION | NO. RESPONSA | NO. WORDS (IN THOUSANDS) |
|---|---|---|---|---|
| 13. R. Betzalel Ashkenazi | R. Betzalel b. Abraham Ashkenazi, c. 1520–1591/4?, Egypt, Israel | Jerusalem, 1968; p.o. Lemberg, 1904 | 41 | 207 |
| 14. *Emunat Shmuel* | R. Aaron Samuel b. Israel Koidonover (also spelled Kaidanover), c. 1614–1676, Poland, Lithuania, Germany | Jerusalem, 1970; p.o. Lemberg, 1885 | 60 | 68 |
| 15. Chacham Tzvi | R. Tzevi Hirsch b. Jacob Ashkenazi, 1660–1718, Germany, Holland | Israel, 1970; p.o. Debrin, 1942 | 245 | 212 |
| 16. *Shevut Ya'akov*, Parts I, II, III | R. Jacob b. Joseph Reischer, c. 1670–1733, Bohemia, Galicia, Germany | Jerusalem, 1972; p.o. Lemberg, 1861 | 551 | 381 |
| 17. Rabbi Azriel (*Orach Chaim, Yoreh De'ah*) | R. Azriel Hildesheimer, 1820–1899, Germany | Tel-Aviv, 1969 | 313 | 178 |
| 18. *Heichal Yitzchak*, Part I (*Even HaEzer*) | R. Isaac Herzog, 1888–1959, Poland, England, Ireland, Israel | Jerusalem, 1969 | 34 | 134 |
| 19. ,, ,, III | ,, | Jerusalem, 1972 | 65 | 93 |
| 20. *Igrot Moshe* (*Orach Chaim*) | R. Moses Feinstein, born 1895, Lithuania, America | New York, 1959 | 192 | 229 |
| 21. ,, ,, (*Yoreh De'ah*) | ,, | New York, 1960 | 260 | 356 |
| 22. ,, ,, (*Even HaEzer*) | ,, | New York, 1961 | 179 | 275 |

| TEXT: RESPONSA OF | AUTHOR | EDITION | NO. RESPONSA | NO. WORDS (IN THOUSANDS) |
|---|---|---|---|---|
| 23. *Igrot Moseh* (*Choshen Mishpat, Orach Chaim* II, *Even HaEzer* II) | R. Moses Feinstein, born 1895, Lithuania, America | New York, 1964 | 247 | 240 |
| 24. " " (*Yoreh De'ah* II, *Orach Chaim* III, *Even HaEzer* III) | " | New York, 1973 | 325 | 322 |
| 25. Mahari Minz | R. Judah b. Eliezer Minz, c. 1408–1506, Germany, Padua | Crackow, 1882 | 15 | 32 |
| 26. Maharam Padua | R. Meir b. Isaac Katzenellenbogen, 1473–1565, Prague, Padua | Crackow, 1882 | 88 | 82 |
| 27. Chatam Sofer, Part VIII (Collected responsa) | R. Moses Sofer, 1762–1839, Germany, Hungary | Chatam Sofer Institute, Jerusalem, 1973 | 121 | 106 |
| | | Total | 5,660 | 7,101 |

# APPENDIX III

## SEARCH TOPICS RUN ON THE COMPUTER

In this appendix, the search topics submitted to the Responsa Project for computerized literature searches are listed. The searches were run on a number of different databases corresponding to the gradual growth of the Project databank, and they are grouped chronologically by the database upon which they were executed. (Note that some of these topics appear several times in the list, as they were re-run upon larger databases.)

Following is a short summary of the databases and the searches run on them:

> *Database I* — 11 experimental searches were performed on the first responsa text computerized by the project: Rivash.
>
> *Database II* — 110 searches were run on a database of 5 responsa collections: Rivash, Rosh, Rashba Parts II, V, and *Meyuchasot* (attributed to Ramban). These include 93 searches which formed the major evaluation test trial of the system, 62 of which were submitted by the Institute for Research in Jewish Law at the Hebrew University (= IRJL).
>
> *Database III* — 102 searches were run on a database of 19 responsa collections (the last three were run on a temporary database of 40 responsa collections).
>
> *Database IV* — 42 searches were run on a database of 52 responsa collections.
>
> *Database V* — 87 searches have been run on the present database of 74 responsa collections (July, 1976).

The search requests were submitted by IRJL, by various Rabbinic and research institutions (in Israel and abroad), by individual scholars and graduate students in Judaica, by members of the Project staff and miscellaneous other sources.

For further information on a number of topics, we have included references to the classic English language work on Jewish Law, *Main Institutions of Jewish Law*, by the former Chief Rabbi of Israel, Rabbi Dr. Isaac Herzog (Soncino Press, London and New York; second edition, 1965, 2 volumes). General information on Jewish Law can be found in the *Encyclopaedia Judaica*. A list of the articles on Jewish Law in the *Judaica*, grouped by the various fields of legal study, is found in *Diné Israel IV* (Faculty of Law, Tel-Aviv University, Tel Aviv, 1973), pp. 273–274.

## Database I

1. Various topics of the occult, in the responsa of Rivash.
2. Marranos of 1391.
3. The intent required on the part of a gift recipient in order to effect transfer of the gift into his ownership.
4. In a case of levirate marriage (*yibum*; see *Deut*. 25:5–10), if a younger brother is willing to enter into the marriage, while an older brother, generally the first in line for *yibum*, wants to grant a formal release from *yibum* (i.e., *chalitzah*), who takes precedence?
5. An engaged couple is found in seclusion together, under suspicious circumstances. Could these be grounds for claiming that the marriage was consummated?
6. In a breach of promise suit, can the breaching party be sued for those expenses laid out by the non-breaching party, for the benefit of the breachers?
7. The validity of a formal act of monetary acquisition performed without benefit of witnesses, when both parties to the act later admit to its having taken place.
8. The weight of expert medical opinion, stating that a given blow was capable of bringing death, against the halachic presumption (*chazakah*).
9. Can a wife appoint an agent to receive her writ of divorce (*get*) from her husband's agent, when the husband has not explicitly dissented from such an arrangement?
10. Can the husband claim, on the basis of his holding of the wife's property, that the property was legally sold to him?
11. The use of the phrase "*mikol makom*" ("however"), for use in a linguistic study.

## Database II

12. In a conflict between performing a given precept and honoring a parent, which is to take precedence?
13. A father contracted with a third party to the effect that his son would perform a given service for the third party. The son knew of the

contract, and began providing his services. Can the son now back out of the contract?

14. The right of a widow to stop collection from the estate by a creditor, by claiming that the properties are necessary for her maintainence.

15. A has stated that B does not owe him anything, and B has denied that statement, can A now claim payment from B?

16. May a widow marry the witness who testified to her husband's death?

17. Is one's right to a given communal post subject to inheritance?

18. A custom obtained locally which prohibited something permitted by the halacha, those maintaining this custom being unaware of its basic permitted nature as set up by the halacha; upon discovering the truth, must the custom be continued?

19. Must a creditor, upon collecting his due from the property of the debtor, create guarantors so that in the event that preferred creditors will subsequently claim, return of the property now being possessed is assured?

20. The right of a communal minority to exclude themselves *a priori* from a given communal enactment, via a declaration to that effect before enactment.

21. The right of a communal minority to exclude themselves *a priori* from a given communal enactment, through an oath taken before enactment, enjoining those taking the oath from following the dictates of the enactment.

22. The right of a communal minority to exclude themselves *a priori* from a given communal enactment by not voicing acceptance ("saying amen") of the binding oath taken by the community to follow that enactment.

23. The right of a communal minority to exclude themselves *a priori* from a given communal enactment by absenting themselves from the meeting wherein the enactment is passed.

24. In collection from a debtor, are bills of debt owed to that debtor subject to collection?

25. The right of A, while holding property of B, to retain that property of B as surety for payment of a debt, not as yet due, owed to A by B.

26. If a woman received a writ of divorce ("*get*") for termination of a marriage which subsequently proved to be unnecessary, as the marriage was null and void *ab initio*, is she nevertheless to be classed a divorcee vis-a-vis the prohibition of a divorcee to a priest ("*cohen*")?

27. A claims money of B, B claims he has already paid. A had previously received a sum of money from B, which in the meantime he had passed on to C (i.e., there is no possessor, in the sense of "possession is nine-tenths of the law"). Upon whom does the burden of proof lie?

28. When does a woman come into her right to the "additional sum" (i.e., that sum above the minimum demanded by the law) promised her in her marriage contract — from the time of betrothal or from the time of completion of the marriage process?

29. What is to be done with money collected for ransoming a captive, when the captive has perished in captivity?

30. One has acquired a "right of usage" ("*chazakah*") towards a certain building which was subsequently razed. Does his right extend to the new edifice, erected on the site of the former, or has it terminated?

31. A debtor has paid one of two (or more) partners the entire sum of money owed to the partnership. Has he fulfilled his obligation?

32. In collection from an estate, which takes precedence — a marriage contract ("*ketubah*") or a creditor?

33. A claims a debt of B, who denies its existence. A brings one witness to the loan, sufficient to force an oath on B. B takes his oath and is freed. A now finds a second witness. Can the two witnesses now be combined to create a proof strong enough so that B can be forced to pay?

34. A Jew, forbidden to lend money at interest, does so under the explanation that this money really belongs to a non-Jew, who is allowed by Jewish Law to lend at interest — is he to be believed and thus not be disqualified to testify in court?

35. In the case of a number of joint debtors, one of whom has had his share of the debt canceled by the other debtors, is the cancelation valid, or does he continue under obligation?

36. During the course of a flight in a supersonic plane towards the west, one can "catch up" with the sun; i.e., after the sun has set in the west and night has set in, by traveling westward at a sufficient speed, one can re-enter the daylight zone. Many religious laws are based upon the astronomical phenomena of day and night — the Sabbath, the Holidays times of prayer, etc. What effect does such a trip have on these laws?

37. Are orphans bound to pay debts incurred by their deceased father, or are these debts nullified with his demise?

38. Is one to be believed in his declaration that certain goods in his possession do not belong to him?

39. What is the amount of maintainence due a widow who has left her deceased husband's domicile after his death, without sufficient justification?

40. Standards are set in the Talmud for removal of certain potential sources of damage from proximity to a neighbor's property. In a given situation, experts ascertain that these standards are not sufficient to prevent damage. Do the classical Talmudic measurements obtain arbitrarily or are the standards evaluated *ad hoc* by the experts to take precedence?

41. Is a creditor entitled to demand of the witnesses present at a loan a writ of testimony verifying the loan?

42. When a court formally validates a bill of debt, do the parties have to be present?

43. In the selling of property from the estate of the deceased for the maintenance of the widow, does a legal guardian have to be appointed by the court to protect the rights of the orphans?

44. Can a witness to a gift empower another party, a non-witness to the transfer, to sign in his stead on the writ of testimony to the act?

45. A member of a partnership borrowed money under circumstances wherein it is unclear as to whether the money was lent to the partnership *per se*, or to the partner as an individual — can the other partners be obligated in this debt?

46. Communal enactments or bans prohibiting polygamy.

47. Communal enactments or bans prohibiting divorcing a wife against her will.

48. A sold a field to B without any explicit guarantee against seizure by a previous creditor of A. Is such a guarantee to be implicitly understood?

49. Are witnesses to an act of bestowal to be considered qualified to testify only if they were formally appointed as such?

50. What is the validity of a court decision granted by a majority of judges, but not in the presence of all the judges?

51. In a divorce suit brought against the husband by the wife, which court is to have jurisdiction — that of the wife's venue or of the husband's?

52. Can a Jew act under power of attorney for a gentile, in claiming a debt owed the gentile by another Jew?

53. A sells a field to B. After acquisition, A's original title to the field comes under contest. Can B demand annulment of the sale on the possibility that the field will be eventually seized by a contestant, and A will then no longer have resources to restore payment to B?

54. An agent makes expenditures in the course of fulfilling his agency and claims reimbursement from his principal. Can the principal exact an oath from the agent as to the amount of expenditures laid out?

55. Is a lessee entitled to sublet the leased property?

56. Can one appointed to the Communal Board of Governors refuse the appointment?

57. Are witnesses to a loan to be considered qualified to testify only if they were formally appointed as such?

58. A performed an act of sale to B. A now wants to annul the sale on the grounds that he was under the legal age of twenty at the time of sale, and produces two witnesses to that effect. B produces two witnesses who testify that A was of legal age at the time of sale. What is the outcome of the sale?

59. Can one be prosecuted for a crime committed by a member of his household?

60. Can a widow claim payment of her marriage contract ("*ketubah*") from the estate, when the witnesses to her husband's death are normally unqualified to testify in monetary cases — being qualified only in cases of establishing death as a special enactment for enabling the surviving spouse to remarry?

61. A claims proof of ownership of a given piece of property on the basis of his possession of that property for three years with no contestment being voiced ("*chazakah*"). B proves that he contested during the three-year period, though not in A's presence. Is B's contestment valid?

62. Can the family of an orphan contest the appointment of a legal guardian for the orphan by the court? Is there a difference between the orphan's maternal or paternal relations?

63. A used a window overlooking the courtyard of B for a number of years, while B was a minor under supervision of a legal guardian. Is the usage-without-protest of that window a proof of B's relinquishing all rights to protest this infringement on privacy?

64. A divorced his wife under threat by the court of imprisonment. However, during the actual divorce act he formally declared that he was acting of free will, not under duress. Is the divorce valid?

65. A compromise was reached, basically due to lack of evidence. Subsequently new proofs were uncovered. Can the compromise be anulled?

66. In such circumstances where qualified properly trained halachic scholars

are lacking to act as judges, can laymen be appointed to the courts; and if so, what are to be their qualifications?

67. In a claim to ownership on the basis of undisputed possession of a piece of property for three years, is such possession sufficient or must the possessor also take an oath to that effect?

68. Is natural death to be considered an *ones* ("a condition generating impossibility of performance"), and if so which category of *ones* (see Herzog, *Main Institutions of Jewish Law*, Vol. II, p. 248–249)?

69. A judge is forbidden to instruct any of the parties to a suit ("Do not act in the fashion of a lawyer"), but is permitted to aid a litigant incapable of formulating his own claims ("Open your mouth for the dumb"). How are these two seemingly contradictory operatives to be harmonized?

70. Can a verdict given by a halachic authority in a specific instance be used as a precedent in subsequent litigation?

71. Is a court to be presumed to have functioned and found without error?

72. A given act was cause for a suit, which was brought to court. Before judgment, the community accepted a given halachic authority or code as final in all matters. Is the given case to be judged according to previous practice or according to the newly accepted authority?

73. What dietary standards are to obtain in a Jewish-owned hotel catering to non-Jewish guests?

74. Are the authorities of the State of Israel allowed to permit exit from Israel to local residents for the sake of touring abroad? The background: The *halacha* does not permit an Israeli resident to leave Israel, except for economic, family or religious extenuating circumstances — the settlement of the land of Israel being viewed as a religious precept.

75. Can an escaped Jewish criminal or suspect claim asylum in Israel?

76. Is an abortion to be permitted on a pregnant woman who was exposed to a disease capable of rendering the resultant child a seriously malformed and malfunctioning being?

77. Does a workers' union have the right to strike, when an arbitration apparatus exists to which they refuse to submit and the goods involved are liable to perish?

78. Is artificial insemination permitted in the case of a married woman receiving semen from a donor not her own husband?

79. Does an estranged wife who has left her husband's domicile during the 12 month cooling-off period preceding divorce have right to main-

tenance from the estate if her husband passes away during that period?

80. In those cases in which the husband can be legally coerced to divorce, does a marriage of doubtful validity receive the same status as those of certain legality?

81. A witness of "low esteem" who is disqualified to testify by Rabbinic enactment — are there any types of cases in which such testimony is admissible?

82. A woman whose motivation for conversion to Judaism is for the sake of marriage with a Jewish man of her choice; do these motives render her acceptance of the precepts of the Jewish religion hypocritical and void?

83. Can one suspected of being a lawbreaker submit testimony in marital or ritual cases?

84. Is the right to lease a house inherited by the heirs of the lessee?

85. In the lease for an apartment was included a clause enabling the lessor to evict the tenant in the middle of the period described in the lease, if the apartment is needed by the lessor personally. If the apartment is sold during the period of occupancy, does the new landlord acquire the said right of eviction?

86. The history of the use of sky-blue dye (*"techelet"*) in the *tzitzit* (see *Num.* 15:37–41), and the *chalazon* fish from which it was produced.

87. In a criminal act involving a number of counts, among which is one resulting in capital or corporal punishment, and one resulting in a monetary ruling, no such double punishment is to be rendered, the capital/corporal chastisement canceling the monetary obligation (*"kam leh be'derabah me'nei"*).

88. The prohibition against polygamy enacted by Rabbenu Gershom, and cases of extenuating circumstances in which the prohibition can be released, especially the procedure of "100 rabbis in 3 countries" signing a writ of permission.

89. Is the claim of the wife that the husband is incapable of consummating the marriage sufficient grounds for coercing the husband to divorce the wife?

90. If the wife refuses to join her husband in his *aliyah* to Israel, is she to be classified a "rebellious wife" (*"moredet"*) with all the attendant penalties?

91. Rabbenu Gershom likewise enacted against the husband's forcing a bill

of divorce on the wife against her will (see above #77). Is an acceptance of a bill of divorce exacted through denying the wife support and marital relations to be classed as invalid by reason of coercion?

92. The obligation on the father to support his children over the age of six.

93. The right of inheritance of a daughter in the presence of a male heir.

94. The validity of a communal enactment passed by the board of governors or by the community *en masse* when a majority of the promulgators do not accept the basics of Jewish Law.

95. In a doubtful case wherein no direct evidence exists, two legal operatives exist: *Rov* ("majority"), i.e., in a majority of cases the given phenomenon is known to occur, and *chazakah* ("presumption"), usually based on a status quo circumstance. In general, *rov* takes precedence over *chazakah*, in cases of conflict between the two. A unique type of *rov* is recorded by the Tosafot (to Niddah 18b, s.v. *lemutei ruba*), in which the statistics are such that the *rov* is defective. Thus this *rov* has enough weight to neutralize the opposing *chazakah*, but not to outweigh it, so that the outcome is indeterminate. Usages of this *rov* are sought.

96. Can a husband be forced to divorce his wife as a result of her claim that he has become "disgusting" to her, or must she furnish evidence to substantiate her claim?

97. Is it permitted to perform an autopsy in the name of medical research even though no emergency exists in the immediate proximity for application of the findings?

98. "Forty days before the creation of the child, a voice goes forth from Heaven and proclaims: 'The daughter of so-and-so shall marry this child' " (Sotah 2).

99. May sealed cans of conserves be opened on the Sabbath (see the discussion on *mustakei* — Betzah 33).

100. If non-kosher meat (i.e., *trefah*) is boiled in a dairy pot which has been used within the previous 24 hours with milk, does the ensuing mixture enter under the prohibition of "milk and meat" ("*basar be'chalav*") so that it is forbidden to derive any benefit from it?

101. If one serves meat to a non-Jew, is he required to observe the *kashrut* law of removing the blood by salting the meat?

102. Does the principle "*sikah mita'am shetiyah*" ("absorption of ointments is comparable to imbibing") obtain for all forbidden substances?

103. Do phylacteries ("*tefillin*") require a single, continuous piece of leather

for the boxes (*"or echad"*), or may the leather be composed of several pieces of leather glued together?

104. After a governmental devaluation of currency, are old debts to be paid according to the new official rate, or the rate obtaining as of the date of the loan?
105. Historical records of loaning at interest to non-Jews as a profession.
106. Linguistic statistics as to the frequency of certain given words in a given vocabulary.
107. The form of charity known as *ma'aser kesafim*, tithing of income.
108. Is an illegal contract, i.e., a contract requiring the performance of an act forbidden by law, binding, if the said illegal act has been performed, so that payment can now be enforced (*"etnan zonah"*)?
109 When R. Isaac bar Sheshet (Rivash) fled to Algeria in 1391, he found indigenous Jewish communities throughout the country, sunk in poverty and ignorance, remnants of once proud Jewish centers. Information as to the history, culture and socio-economic makeup of these communities is sought.
110. Spanish Jewish Communal enactments (until 1492).
111. Musicological material.
112. Legal abandonment of a lost article "is ineffective if it is ascertained from the circumstances of the case or otherwise that at the moment when the finder took possession of the lost object, the owner had not yet become aware of the loss" (*"yeush shelo mida'at"*; Herzog, *Main Institutions of Jewish Law*, Vol. 1, p. 285).
113. Material germane to education in general (*"chinuch"*), and religious education in particular (*"katan ochel nevelot"*).
114. Informers in Jewish communal history (*"malshinim"*).
115. The role secular studies (*"chochmah chitzonit"*) plays in Jewish thought and religion.
116. Material germane to that consecrating vow called *"cherem"* (lit. "banned" for profane use) in which a secular object was donated for Temple or priestly use (see *Levit.* 27:28), and could not be redeemed, as opposed to *"hekdesh"* ("consecrating"), which could be redeemed.
117. The Hebrew phrase *"yesh le-. . . et"*, an idiomatic form of "he has."
118. The Hebrew phrase *"ma'aseh she-. . ."* ("a case occurred wherein . . .").
119. References to the "Jerusalem Translation" of the Pentateuch ("Targum Yerushalmi").
120. The Hebrew demonstrative-pronoun phrase *"et zeh/zot."*

121. Use of the Hebrew terms *"Omnam"*, *"Omnam ken"* ("however", "Is it true?", "great").

## Database III

122. Use of the Israeli place names Tiberias and Sepphoris as place names in the sense of John Doe, for maintaining the privacy of certain relevant facts of court cases.
123. The dance in Jewish life.
124. References to Isaiah 7:14, "A maid shall give birth . . .."
125. References to France and the French.
126. References to "Profane Texts" (*"sepharim chitzonim"*; See Mishnah Sanhedrin 10:1).
127. The blessing *"shehecheyanu"* ("who has given us life").
128. Trade and loans at interest in the responsa of Rabbi Meir (Maharam) of Rotenburg (Germany, 13th century).
129. The German synagogue.
130. Medieval Hebrew mathematical terminology.
131. The *"Bnei Medinah"* (sons of the state) organization found in Medieval Germany.
132. References to the tractate *Nazir*.
133. References to Jesus of Nazereth.
134. References to Rabbi Abraham Ibn Ezra, the famed 12th-century Spanish Jewish Biblical exegete, poet and philosopher.
135. References to the Jerusalem Talmud ("Talmud Yerushalmi").
136. The prohibition of inflicting pain on dumb animals (*"tza'ar ba'alei chayim"*).
137. The policy and procedure of *"mafrishim otam,"* where in certain marital situations the court will issue an "order of separation."
138. Excommunication as a communal sanction.
139. Use of the modern Hebrew name *"chatzil"* for the eggplant.
140. Material on Rabbi Nissim ben Reuven, Chief Rabbi of Barcelona, and Rabbi Joseph ben David, rabbinic appellate court judge of Saragosa in the responsa collection of Rivash (all Spain, 14th century).
141. The law of the rebellious wife who refuses to keep house for her husband (*"moredet mimelachah"*).
142. Was a blessing on the washing of hands after the meal (*"mayim acharonim"*) before reciting the grace after meals ever in vogue?
143. Handshaking (*"tekiat kaf"*) as a mode of conveyance (*"kinyan"*).

144. The German practice of feeding the lender at the expense of the borrower, until the loan has been repaid.
145. Does a son have a right of inheritance to his father's position in the rabbinate?
146. Greekisms in Hebrew.
147. The weight of custom in Jewish Law.
148. Torts caused by a minor.
149. Intermarriage.
150. The Italian rabbinate during the Renaissance.
151. The honorific rabbinic title "*morenu*" ("our teacher").
152. Hebrew phonetics.
153. References to Tunisian Jewry.
154. The modern Hebrew term "*tapuchei adamah*" ("earth apples") used for potatoes.
155. Hebrew paleographical (history of writing) references.
156. The use of the honorific title "*aluf*" ("chief" — see *Gen.* 36:15–43).
157. In a dispute between residents of two different locales, what are the criteria for establishing venue?
158. The institution of the public reading from the scroll of law ("*k'riat haTorah*") in the synagogue.
159. Martyrdom.
160. Matchmaking ("*shadchanut*").
161. The laws of *orlah* ("covered up"), i.e., the first three years produce of a fruit tree being forbidden for use and eating (*Lev.* 19:23).
162. The wearing of a beard among the Jews.
163. Abortion.
164. The creation of an obligation ("*hitchayvut*") whose subject is not a real object ("*davar she'ein bo mamash*").
165. Old age.
166. Techniques for dealing with the educationally handicapped and disadvantaged in Jewish sources.
167. References to the minor *Midrash*, "*Divrei HaYamim Shel Moshe Rabbenu*" ("The Chronicles of Moses").
168. Family purity among the Jews.
169. References to various coins.
170. Blood libels.
171. Citations of the Mishnah.
172. Citations of the Tractate *Terumot*.

173. Holy societies.
174. The binding force of equitable concepts in Jewish Law (*"lifnim miShurat haDin"*; see, comm. R.S.R. Hirsch to *Deut.* 6:18).
175. The source reference of a certain responsum of Rashba cited by R. Joseph Caro in *Bet Yosef.*
176. Jewish communal leadership in the Medieval Islamic world.
177. References to the Midrash *Kohelet Rabbah.*
178. The family name Kalotz.
179. Glass and glassmakers.
180. Zionism in the writings of Rabbi Moses Sofer (Pressburg, 18–19th centuries).
181. Tenant's right (*"chezkat/cherem haYishuv"*).
182. The commandment of "rebuking a wrongdoer" (*"hocheach tochiach"*; see *Lev.* 19:17) as a halachic modular prototype for rehabilitation of criminals.
183. The *Ta'amim* ("musical notation") of the Bible (see Idelsohn, *Jewish Music*, Chapter III).
184. Citations from the *Halachot Gedolot* of R. Yehudai Gaon (R. Shimon Kiara?).
185. Books, booklending, libraries and archives.
186. The *ben sorer u'moreh* ("the disobedient and rebellious son"; see *Deut.* 21:18–21) as a halachic modular prototpye for dealing with juvenile delinquency.
187. The disqualification of witnesses.
188. Washing of the hands before, during and after the meal (*"netilat yadayim"*).
189. Grammar school teachers.
190. War and warfare.
191. Who first coined the classic Hebrew phrase, *"ain simchah keHatarat haSefekot"* — "There is no joy comparable to that of resolving doubts"?
192. Who first coined the classic Hebrew phrase, *"sha'arei haTerutzim lo nin'alu"* — "The gates of rebuttal are never locked"?
193. The definitions of the term *"tiyul"* ("outing, tour, hike, sport, etc.") in halachic literature, and its usages as a halachic factor.
194. Nullification of property liens by consecration (*"hekdesh"*), possession of leavened foodstuffs prohibited on Passover (*"chametz"*) and manumission (*"shichrur"*).

195. Citations of the Bet Shlomo responsa collection of Rabbi Shlomo Dremer (Galicia, Poland; d. 1872).
196. Linguistic statistics — frequency of penult-accented forms (i.e., those words which are accented on the next-to-the-last syllable) in a given vocabulary.
197. Tenant's right (*"chezkat/cherem haYishuv"*).
198. Full intent (*"gemirut da'at"*) in modes of conveyances (*"kinyanim"*) and obligations (*"hitchayvuyot"*).
199. What is the procedure to be followed if a textual error is discovered in the scroll of law during the mandatory public reading in the synagogue service?
200. The uses of the grammatical causative mode (*"binyan hiph'il"*) in the responsa literature.
201. The Austrian custom during the period of the *Rishonim* (until the 16th century).
202. References to Rabbi Shalom ben Isaac Zekel (14th century; Neustadt, Austria; see Michael, *Or Ha-Hayyim*, 1188), the teacher of Rabbi Jacob Moelin (Maharil).
203. Milk of a non-Jew (*"chalav akum"*).
204. Historical materials from the responsa of Rabbi Meir ben Baruch (Maharam) of Rothenberg.
205. The practice of tithing the income for charitable purposes (*"ma'aser kesafim"*).
206. Musicological material.
207. Historical materials from the responsa of the Rishonim (until the 16th century) in Ashkenaz (Germany, France, Austria, Bohemia, Northern Italy, *et al.*).
208. The use of the grammatical simple mode (*"binyan kal"*) in the responsa literature.
209. References to Rabbi Zerachyah HaLevi (12th century, Provence), author of the *Me'orot* supercommentary and strictures to the *Halachot* of Rabbi Isaac Alfasi on the Talmud.
210. History and laws of insurance.
211. *Prosbul*, a formal declaration before the court, empowering a creditor to collect his debts despite the Sabbatical year (*"shmittah"*).
212. The commandment to settle the land of Israel.
213. Jewish apostates.

214. Use of the Hebrew word "*omnam*" (however), alone, and in combination with "*af*" or "*im*" (if).
215. Yiddish and pre-Yiddish dialects in the time of the *Rishonim* (until the 16th century).
216. Re-evaluation of currency.
217. The customs of donkey-drivers and shipowners as binding in commercial law (see B. Baba Kama 116b).
218. The use of the term "*meshubadei haKahal*" ("the servants of the community") in Ashkenazic Jewry.
219. Suspension of prohibitions against non-kosher foodstuffs in time of war (see B. Chulin 17).
220. Glass, glassware and glassmakers.
221. Medieval Hebrew mathematical terminology.
222. Antecedents of various modern Hebrew phrases and terms.
223. Incarceration and prisons.

## Database IV

224. Use of the Talmudic topic, "*zeh neheneh vezeh lo chaser*" ("A benefits, while B sustains no loss"; B. Baba Kama 20–21) as a source of quasi-contract in Jewish Law.
225. The law of the "profaned priest" ("*chalal*"), the issue of a forbidden priestly marriage (see *Levit.* 21:15).
226. The concept of "*ishtarshei*" ("he has profited") as a source of quasi-contract in Jewish Law.
227. Loans-at-interest of money belonging to orphans under care of a guardian.
228. Bans and excommunications.
229. The laws of a half-slave (i.e., a slave belonging to two partners, one of whom had granted manumission).
230. If a husband cannot maintain himself, can his wife be forced to support him from her income?
231. Certain Biblical commandments and prohibitions are undefined in the Biblical text — the definition being left for the Sanhedrin ("*masar haKatuv leChachamim*", "Scripture has given over the matter to the Sages"): What principles apply to this category of the Oral Law?
232. War and warfare.
233. Citations of the Talmud in the responsa literature.
234. The origin of the term "*chamesh megillot*" ("the five scrolls"), used for

five books of the Hagiographa whose reading in the synagogue on various holidays was obligatory — Esther, Lamentations, Ruth, Ecclesiastes and Song of Songs (see Idelsohn, *ibid.*).

235. Insanity, imbecility and other mental defects as recorded in the responsa literature.

236. Elements of self-protection found in the topic *"rodef"* ("a pursuer" is allowed to be killed to save the life of the pursued — see B. Sanhedrin 22b and ff).

237. References to the first three halachic discussions (*"sugyot"*) in tractate Betza.

238. References to the Falasha (black Ethiopian) Jews.

239. Does the general rule "any commandment linked to time does not obligate a woman" also pertain to the counting of the *Omer*?

240. Re-payment of old loans made in currency since devaluated by the government.

241. Tithing of income.

242. Teachers and teaching.

243. The blessing of *shehecheyanu* ("who has kept us in life").

244. Payment of the marriage contract (*"ketubah"*) after devaluation of currency.

245. Old age and the aged — especially institutions for the care of the aged.

246. The culpability of one who leads another into crime.

247. References to *"Shimushei Torah/Tehillim"*.

248. The commandment of *tzitzit* ("fringes") vis-a-vis women.

249. The prohibition: "A man's implements (*"kli gever"*) shall not be on a woman" (*Deut.* 22:7).

250. The prohibition of privacy between a man and a woman not man-and-wife (*"yichud"*).

251. The sending away of the mother bird sitting on her eggs in order to take the eggs (*Deut.* 22:6–7).

252. "Before a blind man you shall not place a stumbling block" (*Levit.* 19:14).

253. Infringements on the prohibition of interest in transactions of sale where payment is made initially while delivery of the goods is at a later date.

254. The renting of real estate.

255. The element of warning (*"hatra'ah"*) prior to the committing of a

criminal act in order to establish prior intent on the part of the perpetrator, thus establishing culpability.

256. The obligation of a married man, enjoined to support his family, to nevertheless continue his religious studies (*"talmud Torah"*).
257. Education, and in particular, methods of motivation.
258. Bastards and bastardy.
259. Artificial insemination.
260. The law of a married woman found with another man in suspicious circumstances.
261. References to the tractate *Ketubot*.
262. Hospitality and guests.
263. Dividing a courtyard owned jointly by a number of householders in the buildings.
264. An agreement void because the subject of the agreement is without substance (*"kinyan devarim"*; see Herzog, *Main Institutions of Jewish Law*, Vol. II, p. 8).
265. The commandment constitutionally investing the Sanhedrin with its power to govern (*"lo tasur"*, see *Deut.* 17:11).

*Database V*

266. Communal enactments prohibiting the importing of meat slaughtered outside the jurisdiction of the community (*"schechutei chutz"*), to insure that the supervision over the slaughtering and the income from the taxes on meat be totally in the hands of communal council.
267. References to tractate *Menachot* in the responsa of Rivash.
268. The dividing of books of Biblical texts held jointly among a number of partners.
269. What conditions are necessary for permitting the razing of a synagogue?
270. The doctrine of Divine Providence.
271. The doctrine of the Divine origin of the Jewish religion.
272. The culpability of a tort inflicted during a period of mass merriment, such as on the feast of Purim or at a wedding.
273. Upon dividing a commonly-owned courtyard, what quality of materials is the standard for the partition to be erected between the newly-created lots in the yard — superior or inferior?
274. The Talmudic discussion: "one who encompasses his neighbor on three fronts . . ." (see B. Baba Batra 4b).

275. Informers within the Jewish community.
276. A "visual tort", i.e., the invasion of privacy caused by a neighbor viewing into one's property, is recognized as a true tort (*"hezek re'iah"*). Is A's ability to overhear the goings-on in B's apartment (*"hezek shemi'ah"*) similarly tortious?
277. Citations to the Jerusalem Talmud ("Talmud Yerushalmi") containing the term *achoti* ("my sister").
278. Can a debtor be presumed to have repaid his loan before the date required in the agreement (see B. Baba Batra 5a)?
279. In the post-Sanhedrin period (the Sanhedrin being the organ of Israel's federal government), can a local rabbinic court impose corporal or capital punishment, usually predicated on the existence of a Sanhedrin, in order to preserve law and order within the local, autonomous or semi-autonomous Jewish community (either in Israel or in the Diaspora)? If so, which forms of punishment are recognized?
280. Are the sages empowered to nullify a marriage?
281. Various Talmudical enactments "for the ways of peace" (*"darchei shalom"*; see B. Gittin 59a).
282. Yiddish and pre-Yiddish dialects in Ashkenaz during the period of *Rishonim* (until the 16th century).
283. References to the first discussions (*"sugyot"*) found in tractate *Ketubot*.
284. The concept of *brit* ("covenant") as a ground for a communal contract at the heart of the communal framework.
285. The land of Israel.
286. Communal enactments.
287. Relief and charity.
288. The Karaites in *halachah*.
289. Tithing of income.
290. "Love thy neighbor as thyself" (*Lev.* 19:18).
291. Hospices and hospitality for guests.
292. The deaf and dumb in *halachah*.
293. The blind in *halachah*.
294. The obligation to immigrate to Israel (*Aliyah*).
295. Any commandment linked to a specific time is not binding upon a woman.
296. The prohibition of leaving the land of Israel.
297. Under what conditions can a criminal after having received his punishment return to his previous status vis-a-vis acting as a communal

functionary or official in a capacity demanding honesty (*teshuvat perek ze borer*)?

298. When a judge is suspicious that the claims and/or evidence presented before him are trumped up, what policy is he to follow?

299. References to the practice recorded by Rama (Rabbi Moses Isserles) in his glosses to Even HaEzer (74:10) where in case of discord between a mother-in-law and daughter-in-law living in the same apartment, a "trustworthy woman" is domiciled with the family to ascertain who is the cause of ill-will.

300. Historical references to drought years and years of plentiful rainfall in Israel.

301. Zionism.

302. Persian Jewry, particularly in the 16th century.

303. Marranos.

304. One who pursues another in the name of mayhem may be stopped in any way possible, including his bodily injury or even death (*rodef*).

305. References to the tractate *Pesachim*, chapter *Arvei Pesachim*.

306. Aliyah to Israel.

307. Can one use a stolen palm branch to fulfill the commandment of the four species (see *Levit.* 23:39–40)?

308. Can one use a dried-out palm branch to fulfill the commandment of the four species (see *Levit.* 23:39–40)?

309. Can one use a stolen tabernacle to fulfill the commandment of dwelling in tabernacles during the holiday of Sukkot (*Levit.* 23:42)?

310. Use of the Hebrew phrase "*al menat*".

311. Buying and lending of books throughout the ages.

312. The law of the land obtains in the rabbinic court.

313. Various defects disqualifying a palm branch for use in the commandment of the taking of the four species (see #130 above).

314. A palm branch taken from a tree consecrated to an idol, for use in the commandment of the taking of the four species (see #130 above).

315. Certain conditions in a citron fruit (*etrog*) disqualifying it for use in the commandment of the taking of the four species (see #130 above), e.g., green color.

316. May a fifth species be added to the above mentioned four species in the name of improving upon the minimum requirements for fulfilling the commandment as recorded in the Bible (*bal tosif*)?

317. Citations of tractate Baba Batra.

318. The law of the land obtains in a rabbinic court.
319. *Halachah LeMoshe MiSinai* ("a law of Moses, from Sinai") — an oral explanation of a commandment recorded in the Pentateuch, having no base for deduction in the written text.
320. The use of the diacritical mark, *sheva*, as designating the absence of a vowel-attachment to a consonant.
321. Liturgical poems, poets, and poetry.
322. Quotations from the commentary of Rabbi Mordechai ben Hillel (Germany, 13th century) to the Talmud.
323. Can the commandment of taking the four species be fulfilled while an interposition (i.e. an intervening object) exists between the species and the hands of the taker?
324. Disqualifying factors of the myrtle branch for the four species.
325. The minimum size of the palm branch.
326. The *Mamran* bill of indebtedness in vogue in Poland and Eastern Europe among Jewish merchants as of the 16th century.
327. No Biblically recorded law is binding unless it post-dates the Giving of the Law on Mt. Sinai (see Yerushalmi Moed Katan 3:5).
328. The covering of the hair by women.
329. The time of day for fulfilling the commandment of taking the four species.
330. The physical taking of the four species.
331. *Kinyan devarim* (see #84 above).
332. Citations of the Talmudic discussions (*sugyot*) from B. Sukkah 38–39.
333. References to Rav Natronai Gaon (Rav Natronai Bar Hilai; Sura, Babylonia, 9th century).
334. References to a type of land-sale in vogue in Spain (until 1492) called "cinch", wherein the buyer agreed to return the land to the seller should the seller procure the necessary funds during a stipulated period of time. This created an interest problem, as the buyer had use of the land and title to its produce during the interim period (see Tur and especially Bet Yosef, Yoreh Deah, beginning of section 174).
335. Is A obligated to endanger his own life in order to save the life of B?
336. The city of Yavne, Israel.
337. The marriage contract (*ketubah*).
338. The syntactic use of the Hebrew word "*vadai*" ("certainly") in the sentence.
339. *Gedolei Ashkenaz.*

340. Suicide in the *halachah*.
341. References to tractate *Chagigah*.
342. The daughter's inheritance in the estate.
343. The kindling of candles to inaugurate the holiday.
344. The custom of reciting the *Hallel* at the evening service (*Ma'ariv*) on the first night of Passover.
345. Matchmaking and matchmakers (*shidduch*).
346. The city of Chevron (Hebron), Israel.
347. Where are children to be placed upon the breakup of a family?
348. "You shall not follow their (heathen) practices" (*Chukot HaGoy*; see *Levit.* 18:3).
349. Euthanasia (mercy killings).
350. Citations of tractate *Gittin*.
351. Citations of tractate *Kiddushin*.
352. References to the Aramaic translations of the Bible.

# APPENDIX IV

## LISTS OF PUBLICATIONS

The lists do not include abstracts, notes, popular expositions or surveys, etc.

A.  PUBLICATIONS DESCRIBING THE RESPONSA SYSTEM

1.  A. S. Fraenkel, "Legal information retrieval," *Advances in Computers* (F.L. Alt and M. Rubinoff, eds.), Vol. 9, Academic Press, Inc., New York, 1968, pp. 113–178.

2.  A. S. Fraenkel, "Modern retrieval methods applied to Jewish case law," *Proc. of First Int. Symp., Soc. of Technical Writers and Publishers*, Tel-Aviv, Dec. 1968, pp. R1–1—R1–9.

3.  A. S. Fraenkel, "A retrieval system for the Responsa," *Proc. Assoc. Orthodox Jewish Scientists*, No. 2, 1968, pp. 3–42.

4.  M. Cohen, "Full-text information retrieval," M. Sc. thesis, Dept. of Math., Tel-Aviv University, 1969, 83 pp. (Hebrew).

5.  A. S. Fraenkel, "Full-text document retrieval," *Proc. Symp. on Information in Chemistry*, Tel-Aviv, May 1969, pp. 86–90.

6.  A. M. Schreiber, "Computerized storage and retrieval of case law without indexing: The Hebrew Responsa Project," *Law and Computer Technology*, 2:11, Nov. 1969, pp. 14–22.

7.  Y. Choueka, M. Cohen, J. Dueck, A. S. Fraenkel, M. Slae, "Full-text document retrieval: Hebrew legal texts," (Report on the first phase of the Responsa retrieval project), *Proc. ACM Symp. on Information Storage and Retrieval* (J. Minker and S. Rosenfeld, eds.), University of Maryland, April 1971, pp. 61–79.

8.  Y. Choueka, M. Cohen, J. Dueck, A. S. Fraenkel, M. Slae, "Full-text case law retrieval: The Responsa Project" (a solicited expanded form of paper no. A–6), *Working Papers on Legal Information Processing Series*, J. Schweitzer Verlag, Berlin, Pamphlet No. 3, 1972, 64 pp.

9.  Y. Choueka, "Fast searching and retrieval techniques for large dictionaries and concordances," *Hebrew Computational Linguistics* (Bar-Ilan University), No. 6, July 1972, pp. 12–32 (Hebrew). English abstract: p. E–33.

10.  M. Slae, "The computer as a tool in 'oral law' research," *Proc. of Conf. on the Oral Law, Torah Shebe'al Peh*, (Y. Rephael, ed.), Mossad Ha-Rav Kook, Jerusalem, No. 14, 1972, pp. 151–155 (Hebrew).

11.  R. Attar, A. S. Fraenkel, Y. Choueka, D. Schindler, "Linguistic files in document retrieval system," *Proc. of the 8th National Conf. of the Inf. Processing Assn. of Israel*, Tel-Aviv, 1972, pp. 218–247 (Hebrew).

12.  A. S. Fraenkel, "Mechanized information retrieval as an auxiliary tool in Jewish law research," *Proc. 5th World Congress of Jewish Studies* (1969), Jerusalem, Vol. 5, 1973, pp. 78–98 (Hebrew). English abstract: p. 68.

13.  M. Slae, "Legal research through computers," *Dine Israel* (Faculty of Law, Tel-Aviv University), Vol. 4, 1973, pp. 233–245 (Hebrew).

14. F. Dreizin, "Concerning the structure of a coherent text on the morphological level," *Hebrew Computational Linguistics* (Bar-Ilan University), No. 8, August 1974, pp. E-9–E-25 (Also: Technical Report No. 2, IRCOL, Bar-Ilan University, 17 pp.)

15. F. Dreizin, "Formulae in coherent text: linguistic relevance of symbolic insertions," *American Journal of Computational Linguistics*, Microfilm No. 14, 1975, pp. 70–85. (Also: Technical Report No. 6, IRCOL, Bar-Ilan University, 31 pp.)

16. S. Spero, Z. Ilani, "The Responsa literature as an aid to teaching Talmud," *Shema'atin*, 13:44, 1975, pp. 14–21 (Hebrew).

17. M. Slae, "Legal research through computers — a progress report," *Diné Israel* (Faculty of Law, Tel-Aviv University), Vol. 6, 1975, pp. 251–282.

18. A.S. Fraenkel, E. Spitz, "Automatic construction of Hebrew concordances with ramifications to English concordances," IRCOL, Bar-Ilan University, Technical Report No. 1, 55 pp.

19. R. Attar, Y. Choueka, N. Dershowitz, A.S. Fraenkel, "KEDMA — Linguistic tools for retrieval systems," IRCOL, Bar-Ilan University, Technical Report No. 4.

20. R. Attar, A. S. Fraenkel, J. Stein, "Local feedback in full-text English and Hebrew retrieval systems," Technical Report No. 5, IRCOL, Bar-Ilan University, 84 pp.

21. R. Attar, A. S. Fraenkel, "Local feedback in full-text retrieval systems," submitted.

22. A. S. Fraenkel, "The Responsa Project — an overview (All about the Responsa retrieval project you always wanted to know but were afraid to ask)," IRCOL, Bar-Ilan University, Technical Report No. 7, 13 pp. To appear in: *Proc. Third Symp. on Legal Data Processing in Europe*, Oslo, July 1975; in *Jurimetrics Journal*, and in *Informaticae Diritto* (in Italian).

23. F. Dreizin, D. Raab, "Towards dynamic representation of sentence meaning," IRCOL, Bar-Ilan University, Technical Report No. 8.

24. F. Dreizin, "Negation: Grammatical, semantical and pragmatic," IRCOL, Bar-Ilan University, Technical Report No. 9.

25. Y. Choueka, F. Dreizin, "Mechanical resolution of lexical ambiguity in a coherent text: Algorithms and experimental results" (extended abstract), IRCOL, Bar-Ilan University, Technical Report No. 10, 4 pp.

26. Y. Choueka, "The Responsa Project: A status report," IRCOL, Bar-Ilan University, Technical Report No. 11.

27. Y. Choueka, A. S. Fraenkel, Y. Pechenick, M. Stae, "The Responsa Project: A — The database," IRCOL, Bar-Ilan University, Technical Report No. 12.

B. RESEARCH IN JUDAICA AND HUMANITIES USING THE RESPONSA MECHANIZED SYSTEM AND DATA-BASE.

1. M. Slae, "References to marranos in the responsa of Rabbi Isaac bar Sheshet, information retrieval by computer," (an expanded form of paper no. B–3), *Bar-Ilan University Year Book* (H. Hirschberg, M. Beer, eds.), Vol. 7–8, 1969; Hebrew section: pp. 397–419, English section: pp. XLVII–LXIV.

2. M. Slae, "The Occult in the Rivash responsa," *Shanah B'Shanah* 5731 (A. Pechenick, ed.), Heichal Shlomo, Jerusalem, 1970, pp. 226–236 (Hebrew).

3. M. Slae, "References to marranos in the responsa of Rabbi Isaac bar Sheshet, information retrieval by computer," *Proc. 5th World Congress of Jewish Studies —* 1969, Jerusalem, 1973, pp. 23–37.

4. S. Deutsh, "The element of *Gemirut Da'at* (firmness of resolution) in conveyances and obligations," Master's Thesis, Faculty of Law, University of Tel-Aviv, 1973.
5. Z. Keren, "Musicological information in the responsa of Rivash, Rosh and Rashba, *Sinai*, Vol. 74, 1973, pp. 81–84 (Hebrew).
6. M. Slae, "Glass in the responsa literature: a study by computer," *Niv-Hamidrashia*, Vol. 11, 1974, pp. 110–119.
7. M. Z. Kaddari, "A study in diachronic Hebrew Syntax," *The Chanoch Yelon Book*, Bar-Ilan University, 1974, pp. 471–498 (Hebrew), English abstract: p. XXX.
8. A. Kasher, "Does every sentence have a deep performative hyperbranch,?" *The Chanoch Yelon Book*, Bar-Ilan University, 1974, pp. 164–211 (Hebrew), English abstract: p. XVIII.
9. M. Corinaldi, "The remedy of temporary separation between husband and wife as reflected in the decisions of the rabbinical courts," *Shenaton Hamishpat Ha'ivri* (M. Elon, ed.), Institute for Research in Jewish Law, Hebrew University, Jerusalem, Vol. 1, 1974, pp. 184–218 (Hebrew).
10. M. Slae, S. Spero, "Topics in the Halakhic literature (Responsa): Tractate Betsah, the problem of *Nolad*," Study-Aid for Students, Responsa Project, IRCOL, Bar-Ilan University, 1975, 13 pp. (Hebrew).
11. B. Schreiber, M. Slae, "Topics in the Halachic literature (responsa): Tractate Baba Batra — level A," Study-Aid for Students, Responsa Project, IRCOL, Bar-Ilan University, 1975, 62 pp. (Hebrew).
12. N. Munk, M. Slae, "Topics in the Halachic literature (responsa): Tracatate Baba Batra — level B," Study-Aid for Students, Responsa Project, IRCOL, Bar-Ilan University, 1975, 37 pp. (Hebrew).
13. C. Omer, "The definition of *Shoteh* (idiot) according to Jewish sources," Publication of the Psychology Department, Bar-Ilan University, 1975 (Hebrew).
14. M. Slae, Book Review of *Insurance in rabbinic law* (by S.M. Passameneck), *Dine Israel* (Faculty of Law, Tel-Aviv University), Vol. 6, 1975, pp. CXXXI–CXXXIX.
15. M. Slae, "Insurance in Halachic sources," IRCOL, Bar-Ilan University, Technical Report No. 3, 77 pp. (Hebrew),
16. M. Slae, "*Tiyul* (promenade) in the Responsa literature," *HaMa'yan*, 16:3, April 1976, pp. 17–35 (Hebrew).
17. N. Munk, B. Shreiber, M. Slae, "Topics in the Halakhic literature (Responsa): Tractate Sukkah, Chapter *Lulav Hagazul*," Study-Aid for Students, Responsa Project, IRCOL, Bar-Ilan University, 152 pp. (Hebrew).
18. Z. Ilani, "Citation index for tractate Ketubot," A. Rubinstein, Bnei-Brak, 1976.

# DEATH IN LIFE: TALMUDIC AND LOGOTHERAPEUTIC AFFIRMATIONS

REUVEN P. BULKA

In spite of all the sophistication of a highly technologized 20th Century, man has essentially still not come to grips with the psychologically traumatic and emotionally enervating experience of death. To be sure, one finds the odd intellectual or the odd man-in-the-street who is philosophical about death, who is ready, so to say, to live with death. In the main, however, the average man still fears death, the process of dying, and the experiencing of death. Perhaps it should be this way. Perhaps it is ridiculous for philosophers and psychologists to attempt pseudo-explanations which explain, even explain away, death. Perhaps it is the height of obscenity to reduce what is assuredly an awesome reality into an acceptable experience. Then, too, it is possibly self-contradictory for man to, at one and the same time, glorify life and accept death. After all, if life is so valuable, and human existence so beautiful, death should be avoided. And, even though death cannot be avoided in fact, it can be avoided in mind. Taking into consideration man's preoccupation with life, it is to be expected that thoughts of death should be suppressed. The thought of death having been suppressed, man becomes psychologically unequipped to face death when death confronts him.

If what we have said is true, then the secularized 20th Century technology as a creeping philosophy does not enhance but rather exacerbates the problem. Man's cold and calculated sophistication, designed to mediate between man

*Rabbi Dr. Reuven P. Bulka is the rabbi of Congregation Machzikei Hadas, Ottawa, Canada. He received his Ph.D. degree from the University of Ottawa in 1971, concentrating on the Logotherapy of Dr. Viktor E. Frankl. Dr. Bulka is the author of* The Wit and Wisdom of the Talmud, *and co-editor with Dr. Joseph Fabry and Dr. William Sahakian of the forthcoming volume*, Logotherapy.

*Dr. Bulka is also the founder and editor of the newly-launched* Journal of Psychology and Judaism. *He has contributed scholarly articles to various journals, including Chronicle Review, Jewish Digest, Jewish Life, Jewish Spectator, Humanitas, The Journal of Ecumenical Studies, The Journal of Religion and Health, and Tradition.*

and nature in a this-wordly setting, almost totally ignores what may be called "the ultimate problems of man's being." The concerns of a dubious tomorrow are muted in the obsessive preoccupation with today. And, as long as death and what follows death are relegated to the "tomorrow," the "today" world will find it increasingly difficult to properly understand death.

What is needed to deal with the problem on a meta-clinical level is an acceptable philosophy of life which fuses together the today and tomorrow, a philosophy which goes beyond the "as if" of a Camus but is more livable than the *Sein-zum-Tode* of a Heidegger. If the today and tomorrow can be shown to be intermingled and intertwined, then perhaps the philosophical problems of death can be tackled. The hope is that the psychological aspect would follow.

# I

In attempting to formulate a philosophy of life and death to deal with the aforementioned problems, the present paper will present two traditions, one religious, the other secular, relating to the role of death in life. The religious tradition is that found in the Talmudic and Midrashic literature of Judaism. The secular tradition is the logotherapy of Viktor E. Frankl.

Even a cursory glance at the legislative structure of Judaism indicates an appreciation for life. With few exceptions, man is, in Judaism, at all times excused from the performance of a commandment when this endangers his life.[1] Danger to life suspends the code of Jewish existence. According to some,[2] this does not even allow man the possibility of being a theological hero. He must suspend religious observance for the higher reality, life itself. At the same time, the attitude to death in Judaism is a surprisingly positive one. Midrashic comment on the verse, "And God saw everything that he had made, and behold, it was very good" (Genesis 1:31) suggests that "very good" can be equated with death.[3] In a similar vein, it is said of the psalmist David that "He looked upon the day of death and broke into song."[4] At once, we are thus confronted with an affirmative attitude to life and a positive outlook to death. In simple terms, the two ideas can be reconciled with the mediating principle that man would not be faced with an imperative to act and accomplish if his life were endless. That his existence may be terminated suddenly is a reality which forces, or should force, man to utilize his allotted moments as meaningfully as possible.

It seems, though, that awareness of death in the abstract is not deemed enough to act as imperative. Thus, to prevent transgression, the Talmud proposes that man be mindful, among other things, of where he is eventually going, to a place of dust, worms, and maggots.[5] Of the righteous it is said that they "... set their death in the forefront of their thoughts."[6] And a famous sage, to bring home the importance of awareness of death, suggested to his disciples that they repent one day before their death. Immediately he was confronted with the expected question, does then man know on what day he will die?, to which the sage responded, "Then all the more reason that he repent today, lest he die tomorrow, and thus his entire life is spent in repentance."[7] Repentance here is presented in the existential sense, as the constant process of investigating the past to improve the future. In any event, we have here an ancient thought system which correlates the fact of death with meaningful life. Admittedly, there is a danger in proposing an extreme such as constantly being mindful of death, which can easily give birth to neurotic behavior. It would be more realistic to take this extreme as a counter to the extreme of neglect, with man in his own unique situation striking a delicate balance. The balance might rest in the awareness of death when establishing the "game-plan" for life, and in investing one's life energies in carrying out the plan.

The paradoxical nature of man's relation to death is best expressed in a dialogue between Alexander of Macedon and the elders of the south city.

> He said to them: What shall a man do to live? They replied: He should mortify himself. What shall a man do to kill himself? They replied: He should keep himself alive.[8]

A Midrashic counterpart of the same idea is the following: "Death is near to you and far from you, as well as far from you and near you."[9] The more man is interested merely in keeping himself alive, the more he cuts himself off from meaningful living. In the pursuit of years he wastes the days. The more man realizes he is mortal, destined to die, the more he will try to accomplish, thus perhaps even gaining immortality. Basic to the Talmudic approach is the inherent notion that death, properly understood, can be a vital life force. Needless to say, the element of fear can easily enter into the religious sphere, as when man is urged to behave in life because of the consequences he might face afterwards. Such a confrontation with life and death out of fear, which might yield positive results on a quantitative level, nevertheless falls short on the qualitative level. To propose transcending death in an atmosphere of fear is to circumvent the trauma of death with an even greater dis-ease, the life lived in fear. An affirmation of the role of death in life on an existential level would thus seem to be most appropriate. For this, we turn to the existential philosophy underlying the logotherapeutic system of Viktor E. Frankl.

## II

Logotherapy is the school of psychotherapy fathered by Frankl and focusing on the importance of meaning in life. Logotherapy proposes the existence of unconditional meaningfulness and posits the notion that man's primary motivational force is to find meaning in life.[10] Logotherapy, unlike other existential systems, is basically an optimistic, future-oriented system, focusing on man's freedom and the multitude of possibilities for man to find meaning. Logotherapy carefully avoids injecting such ideas as fear, trembling, sickness-unto-death, nausea, anxiety, etc., into the human situation. Instead, ideas such as hope, meaning, joy, ecstasy, and values form its basic lexicon. Nevertheless, logotherapy does not recoil from facing squarely the issues of suffering and death.

The process of death, according to Frankl, is not a severed fragment of the human biography. Death is part of life. "Without suffering and death human life cannot be complete."[11] In projecting the notion of "unconditional meaningfulness," man is called upon to elicit meaning up to and including the moment of death. For ". . . human life, under any circumstances, never ceases to have meaning, and this infinite meaning of life includes suffering and dying, privation and death."[12] The thesis of logotherapy is that man is to live, and die, meaningfully.

So much for the moment of death. What bearing does the inescapability of death have on life itself?

Frankl believes the fact of death is crucial to life; ". . . only in the face of death is it meaningful to act."[13] Contrary to the thought that death indicates the futility and meaninglessness of life, Frankl asserts that if man's life tenure were really infinite in duration, he could continually, and legitimately, postpone every action forever. It would not really matter whether a deed was performed now, or ten years from now. "But in the face of death as absolute finis to our future and boundary to our possibilities, we are under the imperative of utilizing our lifetimes to the utmost, not letting the singular opportunities — whose 'finite' sum constitutes the whole of life — pass by unused."[14] In a word, man exists in time and time exists in man. In the becoming process, the man-time combination is utilized. The death of man in time signifies the passing of a life. The death of time in man signifies the passing of a moment. Ultimate death is only a more radical form of expiration, more radical than the death in installments involved in the wasting of time.

On the other hand, proper utilization of time signifies a positive irreversibility, for that which has been accomplished remains as a reality forever. Transitoriness applies only to the potentialities, which, once actualized, are, so to say, "rescued . . . into the past."[15] Death poses a constant imperative to man, an imperative which says that each moment, as life itself, is irrepeatable, and must be utilized. Death makes life meaningful. The challenge of life is how to use each moment, which values are to be actualized, and which doomed to non-existence.[16] In logotherapy this is taken to indicate the importance of the past, that ". . . man's past is his true future."[17] The past deeds are "safely stored," immune from any erasure. And, for the dying man who has no future, the past, which is really his life, is the eloquent testimonial to his existence. Death ends the becoming process. In death man "is." And he "is" what he was in life.[18]

Ironically, Frankl, to counter the negativism usually linked to the fact of death, actually introduces the ubiquity of death even in life, in the passing of time, as a counter to nihilism. The fact that not only life, but also the moment can be lost, and are in fact irreversible, leads to the logotherapeutic notion of man's responsibleness in life. For, if what has been done can forever be undone, and vice versa, then virtue and vice would disappear in uncertainty, praise and blame would be impossible and education unmanageable. Human beings would be free from the responsibilities which underlie their humanness. Responsibleness is a responsiveness to the challenges posed by life, challenges which call for undelayed response. If the existence of man in time is "temporality" and the existence of time in man is "singularity," the following statement capsules these ideas: "The meaning of human existence is based upon its irreversible quality. An individual's responsibility in life must therefore be understood in terms of temporality and singularity."[19]

Irretrievability of a past moment, singularity, and of a past life, temporality, constitute the basis of human existence, and are the impetus for man's responsibleness to life. Frankl thus sees death as an ongoing life process, not in the pessimistic sense, but in the positive sense. Just as total death, the death of man in time, challenges man's life in its totality, so fragmentary death, the death of time in man, challenges man in each moment. The sum of these moments constitutes the existence of man.

### III

It is instructive at this point to note the striking similarities between the Talmudic and logotherapeutic attitudes to death. Although they are separate systems, the one religious, the other secular, nevertheless both take an affirmative attitude to death. The affirmative attitudes are no doubt born of differing assumptions. At work in the Talmud is the fundamental faith that God would not have put in the world a purely negative reality or fact of life. This is not to glorify or seek death, rather to indicate that death enhances the human situation. In logotherapy one senses an optimism with life which is, at once, a philosophical and psychological proposition. As death is unavoidable, it is psychologically silly and philosophically untenable to deny its importance. And, to avoid the dangers of negativism, which can only impede the human situation, it is vital to say yes to life in its totality. Even if life appears senseless, and death more than meaningless, it is vital for man to make life and death as meaningful as possible, to make life philosophically justifiable and psychologically livable. In both these systems, there is an inherent affirmation of the natural order, and an implicit faith in all life contingencies.

In a sense, one may argue that logotherapy presents nothing new, taking into account the fact that its ideas already appeared centuries ago in the Talmud. Then, too, the affirmative attitude to death is already found in the writings of so many existential thinkers. Perhaps the uniqueness of the logotherapeutic approach is that it is so affirming while being a secular system, and is affirming with a positive and realistic bent.

For the man-in-the-street, theological or logical propositions are not likely to evoke any excitement. Theology and philosophy have a habit of finding the ear of few people. If Hegel is correct in saying history is what man does with death, then the 20th Century poses a unique challenge. Some see in the proliferating abundance of life-saving techniques and their use on the dying person a denial of the individual's right to his own death.[20] It is almost as if science is doing its utmost to see if it can beat the death force, if it can conquer nature. And, ironically, the same medical prowess which tries to conquer death is the judge of when medicine can no longer help, when the situation is hopeless to the point that euthanasia is indicated. In these attitudes one senses a trend to deny nature, to let medicine prolong, and, if need be, to terminate. The affirmative view of logotherapy is consistent when it asks if ". . . we are ever entitled to deprive an incurably ill patient of the chance to 'die his death,' the chance to fill his existence with meaning down to its last moment . . ."[21] For, "The way he dies, insofar as it is really his death, is an integral part of his life, it rounds that life out to a meaningful totality".[22]

Perhaps what we should be arguing for is a return to nature, to an awareness and appreciation of the natural, unavoidable aspects of human existence. Feifel hints at this when he argues that ". . . the concept of death must be integrated into the self to subdue estrangement from the fundamental nature of our being."[23] Frankl alludes to it when he asserts that "this acceptance of finiteness is the precondition to mental health and human progress, while the inability to accept it is characteristic of the neurotic personality."[24]

In the striving for an orderly, structured world, a world of rules and clear-cut patterns which are undoubtedly necessary for technology to benefit the masses, the matter of death has suffered the fate that is to be expected when eschewing the inevitable.

The ultimate answers relative to the problem are not logical but paradoxical. From the Talmudic dialogue previously cited to the effect that to live one must mortify himself and to die one should indulge in life, to the Heideggerian idea that one can conquer death by actually willing it, to the logotherapeutic notion that to the extent which man understands his finiteness he also overcomes it,[25] it is evident that man magnifies the problems of death by avoidance, and counters these problems by accepting and affirming the role of death in life. In espousing an affrmative attitude to the natural order, it might be possible not only to effectively overcome the trauma associated with death, but also to re-enter into meaningful dialogue with life, and to project human concerns into the forefront of man's endeavors.

# REFERENCES

1. The Babylonian Talmud, *Yoma*, 85b.
2. Maimonides, *The Foundations of Torah*, 5:4.
3. Midrash Rabbah, *Genesis*, 9:5.
4. The Babylonian Talmud, *Berachoth*, 10a.
5. The Babylonian Talmud, *Abot*, 3:1.
6. Midrash Rabbah, *Ecclesiastes*, 7:9.
7. The Babylonian Talmud, *Shabbat*, 152a.
8. The Babylonian Talmud, *Tamid*, 32a.
9. Midrash Rabbah, *Ecclesiastes*, 8:17.
10. Viktor E. Frankl, *Man's Search for Meaning* (New York: Washington Square Press, 1968), p. 154.
11. *Ibid.*, p. 106.
12. *Ibid.*, pp. 131–132.
13. Viktor E. Frankl, *Psychotherapy and Existentialism* (New York: Simon and Schuster, 1968), p. 30.
14. Viktor E. Frankl, *The Doctor and the Soul* (New York: Bantam Books, 1967), p. 52.
15. *Psychotherapy and Existentialism*, p. 30.
16. *Man's Search for Meaning*, p. 191.
17. Viktor E. Frankl, "Time and Responsibility", in *Existential Psychiatry*, Vol. 1, 1966, p. 365.
18. *Ibid.*
19. *The Doctor and the Soul*, p. 52.
20. Elisabeth Kübler-Ross, *On Death and Dying* (New York: Macmillan, 1970), pp. 8–9.
21. *The Doctor and the Soul*, p. 37.
22. *Ibid.*
23. Herman Feifel, "The Problem of Death" in Hendrik M. Ruitenbeek (ed.), *Death: Interpretations* (New York: Dell Publishing Co., 1969), p. 129.
24. *Psychotherapy and Existentialism*, p. 47.
25. *Ibid.*, p. 36.

# MA'ASEH BERESHITH
## (Original Creation)
# AND GEOLOGY

### Hugo Mandelbaum

"As a person close to research in geology and paleontology I have no doubt whatsoever that there is no possibility to explain the existence of the world within a duration of 5728 years, whatever assumption science may take" (Wuerzburger, *Hamayan* V:8, p. 80).

The question, whether one who believes in *Torah min Hashamayim* (Torah from Heaven) can underwrite the above quotation, has been raised time and again. In the recently published book *Challenge*, there is an anthology of quotations (p. 124 ff.) from midrashic and other sources, including quotations from Rambam, Tifereth Israel, Rav Kook, and Rav Dessler, which discuss this question.

## Interpretation of the first chapter of Genesis

My first thesis is that the first chapter of Genesis cannot be interpreted as a sequence of statements having as subject matters phenomena known as objects of natural sciences. For instance, according to the mentioned sources, the word *Yom* (literally: day) does not mean the 24-hour rotation of the earth

*Hugo Mandelbaum Ph.D. studied mathematics, geography and geology at Hamburg University where he received his masters and doctoral degrees. He was the founder and, for many years, President of the Detroit branch of the AOJS until his Aliyah in 1971. He currently serves as a member of the Editorial Board of the* Proceedings of the AOJS. *Dr. Mandelbaum retired in 1971 as Professor of Geology at Wayne State University and now resides in Jerusalem.*

*Dr. Mandelbaum's paper elicited considerable discussion among several reviewers. It may be hard to justify the need for a discussion of the status of various geometries or the relationship between mathematical and scientific induction as a preliminary for advancing the suggestion that the universe is designed. Nevertheless, we are publishing this paper but point out that the views are those of the author and do not necessarily represent those of the AOJS.*

on its axis but a time unit on a divine scale. This is the understanding we can call *Peshat* (simple interpretation). Etzion (*Hamayan*, Vol. 8, No. 4, p. 36) objects to this approach on the following grounds: The sources quoted in *Challenge* want to explain the concept of *Yom* in a transposed sense (*Lo Kipeshutam*); but there is no proof that they interpret the concept *only* in a transposed sense, a time period of more than twenty-four hours. However, Etzion's objection is not valid since *Yom* cannot mean both 24 hours *and* more than 24 hours. Hence, the quoted sources understand their interpretation as *Peshat*. The *real* meaning of *Yom*, to them, is a period of more than 24 hours. Alternatively, the meaning of *Yom* may be found on an entirely different level, a spiritual level, so to speak, because it is the basis for *Kedushath Shabbath* (Holiness of the Sabbath) which can also not be understood on a physical level (level of *Derash* or abstract meaning).

"He decided — owing to the immensity and subtlety of the subject matter, added to the deficiency of our understanding — to communicate them [the words of Torah] to us in the form of allegories, hidden sayings, and veiled words . . . yet He enabled ordinary people to make some sense of the words, according to the extent of their understanding and the weakness of their imaginative power" (*Rambam*, Introduction to *Moreh Nevuchim*, quoted from the translation in *Challenge*, p. 128). *Ramban*, in the introduction to his commentary on the Torah (ed. Mossad Harav Kook, 5719, p. 6), states: "All this [astronomical details, location of stars, biology of animals and plants, psychology of man] King Solomon knew [out of his study of the Torah] and he found all in it, in its explanations, its detailed investigations, in its letters and in its detailed forms." Obviously this is neither *Peshat* (literal meaning) nor *Derash* (abstract meaning), but *Remez* (hints) and *Sod* (secret tradition). We common mortals cannot hope to extract such knowledge from the literal form of Scripture. For us to admit ignorance and lack of understanding does not reflect negatively on our belief that the message which the first chapter of Genesis wishes to transmit is of profound importance to our concept of *Torah min Hashamayim*. Such a stand relieves us from a confrontation between our understanding of the physical world (whatever that might be) and the real meaning of the words in *Ma'aseh Bereshith* (Original Creation) (which we admit that we do not know).

I am convinced that any attempt to interpret the meaning of some phrases by physical entities will fail. Such attempts have failed in the past, and attempts in that direction at present fail to be convincing. In support of this statement I will cite a few examples. *Rambam* explains the second verse of

Genesis: "The *earth* was void and empty and *darkness* on the surface of the *water* and the *wind* of . . ." in the following way: What you should recognize is that the four elements . . . are mentioned immediately after the noun *Shamayim* (Heaven) . . . *Choshech* (darkness) is the elementary fire (*Moreh Nevuchim*, 2:30). *Rambam* obviously feels it necessary to mention the four elements of Aristotelian natural philosophy in *Ma'aseh Bereshith*. But what shall we do today at a time when we have knowledge of more than 100 elements and several scores of elementary particles? Is the following question not justified: where in *Ma'aseh Bereshith* do we find an expression of the complicated composition of created matter? Surely *Rambam*'s answer in his time is not acceptable today, nor was it part of the truth at any time.

"Let there be an extension in between the water" (Genesis, 1:6). *Ralbag* (*Sefer Milchamoth Hashem*, 1:5) explains this verse in the following manner: "Water is that material element which does not preserve its outward shape (has no shear resistance). It is placed between some of the heavenly spheres and others. It causes the motion of the upper spheres not to be transmitted to the lower spheres and vice-versa. This (material) is called *Mayim* (water) in this chapter, because of its similarity to the ether, namely the lack of preservation of form."

In this explanation of *Ralbag* we find four concepts of Aristotelian natural philosophy: 1) The heavenly bodies are attached to spheres. 2) Between the spheres is ether, because completely empty space is inconceivable (*horror vacui*). 3) This material must have the hypothetical property of having no shear resistance. 4) There is no distant interaction between material bodies without interconnecting material.

The meaning of words in *Ma'aseh Bereshith* can be found neither in Aristotelian language nor in the language of present-day science. In this respect, I again quote *Ralbag*: "Let there be *light* (Genesis 1:3). This light is the world of the angels, which is the *light* on the basis of *Da'ath Ha'emeth* (the essential Truth) . . . They all agree that this *light* is not a material light, the light of our senses, but, in their opinion, it is an abstract light."

In contrast to this explanation of *Ralbag*, Schwab (*Challenge*, p. 167) tries to restore a physical meaning to the concept *light*. "The light was real in the sense that it was incorporated into the reality of the physical universe . . . light was first intermingled with darkness . . . not an absence of light, but a created darkness . . . Maybe it was akin to what scientists call a concentration of cosmic dust, dark nebulae or the like." *Erev* (evening) is called when *light* was partly obscured by some dark matter. When the Creator separated the light from this peculiar darkness, there was *boker* (morning). . . . Here is a cosmic time system (the time it takes the creation light to appear and fade away) which came into existence simultaneously with the creation of the universe . . . and continued as long as the universe will last." If Schwab refers to cosmic dust, nebulae or the like, why not go further and mention "black holes" (see R. Penrose, "Black Holes," *Scientific American*, May 1972) as an explanation for *Choshech* (darkness)?

Even if we would know what dark nebulae, or black holes are, how could such a "time system" work? To which longitude on earth would it be geared? It seems absurd to postulate a cosmic phenomenon without any physical law timed to a miniature scale of a daily rotation of the earth. Unless, of course, the appearance of the "creation light" is elevated on a spiritual level, where *Ralbag* placed it.

There are many concepts which defy a clear cosmological explanation. Even the term *Shamayim* (heaven) falls in this category, unless we accept it as meaning the realm of *Malchuth Shamayim* (the divine sphere). What is *Tohu vavohu, Choshech, Ruach Elokim, Raki'a, mayim me'al laraki'a*, etc.? Unless we look for the meaning of these words in the Midrash, no satisfactory cosmological explanation has been (and I add, can) be found. We must accept the fact that the lack of definition is intentional, either because it is not necessary, or the *Peshat* is on a higher level, accessible only to an elite of men. Why not accept this state of affairs and admit: *Amukah v'hi rechokah mimeni* (It is too deep and removed from me)?

*How* the world was created is not related in specific detail in the Torah. The Torah does not tell us about the composition of matter, of molecules, atoms, protons, electrons, neutrons, etc., nor does it tell us about atomic energy and radioactive processes, nor of the whole spectrum of electromagnetic energy, etc. Man was endowed by the Creator with a tool, his *Neshamah* (soul), not only to be able to accept Him as *Melech Ha'olam* (King of the Universe), and to be able to choose between good and evil, but also to be able to discover God's law in nature. Any lack of understanding in the latter sphere does not require atonement. Hence, no harm befalls man if the working of the universe is not revealed to him, and if he fails to recognize it. But if he is able to invent mathematics, to conduct complicated and sophisticated experiments, he has proved one of the fundamentals of the first chapter of Genesis: *Ki Betzelem Elokim bara eth Ha'adam* (He created man in His image; see H. Mandelbaum, "Torah, Facts and Conclusions," *Proc. AOJS*, vol. 1, p. 65).

An objection has been raised against the claim that we cannot derive cosmological facts through an interpretation of the first chapter of Genesis. If we can squeeze meaning even from a single letter of any *halachic* portion of Torah, why should we not try at least to gain as much meaning as possible from the first chapter? The comparison is not valid. We have the thirteen *Midoth she'Hatorah Nidresheth Bahem* (exegetic rules for the *halachic* interpretation of Torah) but we do not have such rules for *Ma'aseh Bereshith*. We are ignorant even of the meaning of the most basic terms. We have good reason to believe that the *real* meaning of *Ma'aseh Bereshith* is the foundation of our faith in the Creator. Why then try to find a meaning on a level for which it probably was not intended, especially in the face of failures of such attempts in the past and in the present?

*Summary*: The Torah did not reveal any scientific facts of cosmology. Such revelation was not necessary for Torah, a regulation of human conduct. We are allowed (and required) to investigate. We do not need to find confirmation of scientific discoveries in the literal sense in the words of *Ma'aseh Bereshith*.

## Possible reasons for the lack of scientific details

*Ramban*, at the beginning of his commentary to the Torah, writes: *Rashi* said that the Torah should have started with the first commandment, *Hachodesh hazeh lachem* (Exod. 12:1) which commands the preparing of the *Korban Pessach* (Passover sacrificial lamb). But, counters *Ramban*, it was necessary for the Torah to start with *Bereshith Bara* (In the beginning God created) as this is the root of our faith ... But *Ma'aseh Bereshith* is a deep secret which cannot be understood from the literal meaning of the verses ... Since this is the state of affairs, *Rashi* was correct, continues *Ramban*, when he stated that there was no need to start with *Ma'aseh Bereshith*, because all this cannot be completely understood from the written word.

To the above we may add another argument. The Torah speaks in terms of human language. It is impossible to explain the laws of the universe, as we understand them today, without the language of mathematics. The language of present-day physics is differential equations. The Torah does not speak in this language, nor could it be understood by Israel at the time of the giving of the Torah, nor by most people nowadays.

## The Foundation of Mathematics, the tool to interpret scientific facts

A confrontation of science and Torah obviously has two fronts. We have tried, in the previous section, to solve the problem by stating that the first chapter of Torah cannot be interpreted as containing scientific facts. The problem is solved by others who state that science cannot produce reliable statements. Y. R. Etzion, in his several-part article on "The Theory of Evolution" (*Hamayan*, Vol. 8, No. 1 to 4) provides a scholarly argumentation against the validity of the theory of evolution, by showing that all its basic assumptions are not valid. However, he goes far beyond that, by stating that all sciences, including and especially mathematics, cannot be relied upon to produce true statements, since they are all based on arbitrary assumptions which either cannot be proven or need no proof. Since he throws mathematics and physical sciences into the same pot, and wants to prove the arbitrariness of the axioms of science on the state of affairs in the field of axiomatics of geometry, it is necessary to counter a few of his misconceptions. Etzion argues that since we now have three valid geometries, Euclidian and two non-Euclidian, and only one can be true, we can see that the arbitrary acceptance or rejection of Euclid's axiom of parallels leads to results that cannot be relied upon to be true scientific facts. This is a complete misinterpretation of the nature of the axioms of mathematics and the development of mathematics that led to non-Euclidian geometry.

To be useful as foundations, axioms of mathematics have to pass a rigorous test. They must be consistent, independent, and complete. They are not assumptions that have no factual validity (Y. R. Etzion, *Hamayan*, Vol. 8, No. 1, p. 22), but are the very building stones with which the structure of mathematics is erected. The axioms define the concepts used by the mathematician. For instance, geometry deals with points, lines and planes. But such entities do not exist in the real world. A real point has three dimensions, a mathematical point has none. These concepts exist in the abstract only and need precise definition. The set of the three axioms of plane projective geometry may serve as an example. Axiom one defines a point: Two lines always lie (intersect) on one point and one point only. Axioms two and three define a line: Two points always lie on one line and one line only (i.e. between two points only one line can be drawn). At least three points lie on a line. It is immaterial then what is meant by point and line, as long as two objects fulfill the above relationships. For instance, we could equate point = line and vice-versa and obtain valid statements, as one can readily see if one copies the above axioms but replaces the word "point" with "line," and vice-versa.

It was precisely at this point that Euclid and those who followed him were in error. The validity of the axioms is not based on the fact that they are a parallel to facts of the real world. It is because no one could assert that at the inaccessible infinite distance in the real world two parallels do not actually interesect that mathematicians tried to prove this fact from the other Euclidian axioms which could be "shown" to be valid in the real world, until Lobashevsky proved that the axiom of parallels is "independent," i.e. is not a consequence of the other axioms. Complete and consistent geometries can be constructed without it (see the example of projective geometry mentioned previously) or with an axiom that has a contrary content (non-Euclidian geometries).

If that is the case, the following question arises: The axioms of mathematics (and not only those of geometry) deal with abstract concepts, which have no counterpart application to things real. Wherefrom do we take the audacity to apply concepts which are but the fruits of our abstract thinking, and the theorems derived from them, to a world that exists outside our brain, over which we have no control, whereas we exercise absolute control in the formulation of the axioms of mathematics? We have complete confidence that this application is justified and that predictions of events in the real world on the basis of applied mathematics are absolutely reliable. Here is a striking example of the overbearing confidence that the world is subject to "our" physical laws, based on mathematical formulation. On the basis of Newton's formulation of the law of gravity and treatment by the method of calculus, we calculate the orbits of planets and predict their exact location at any given time. We do not even wonder why the star does exactly what Newton's law commands. On the contrary, if we find a planet not at its calculated place, we do not find anything wrong with "our" law or our calculations. Something must be wrong with the planet. We calculate the exact location of a body that "must" have disturbed that planet, direct our telescope to that spot in the sky, and discover there and then the heretofore unknown planet Pluto. Wherefrom do we get this absolute faith in our own brain-child? How can we explain the complete parallelism? Philosophy has not as yet found a satisfactory answer to this question. To those who believe in the Creator of this world the answer is given. The One who sets the laws of heaven and earth has endowed man with a divine soul. God has created both, the external and the internal world. Order and law are the basic constituents of the human brain and of the world which we observe. He who put law and order into the *Toho Vavohu* (emptiness and nothingness) of the world gave us the key instrument to unravel the secrets of His universe, so

that we can recognize that "His greatness and His goodness fill the world."
We are not even surprised by the greatest wonder of all, that we are able to
recognize "the wonders that surround us every day."

## The assumptions and the law of induction in science

In contrast to the axioms of mathematics which do not require applicability
to the physical world as proof of their correctness, the assumptions for the
explanation of physical facts and observations have to be proven correct
or wrong by every new fact or every new observation. In the more complex
settings of science today, we speak of a "model" in the mind of the searching
scientist, on the basis of which he constructs experiments, directs his observations and makes his calculations. That "model" will stay unchallenged until
some fact is discovered that contradicts it, or at least requires its modification.
However, there are some basic assumptions whose truth or reliability can
never be proven or disproven. One of these is the principle of induction:
What can be shown to be correct in *all* instances, where applied, is considered
correct in *all* instances. The concept "all" includes instances at inaccessible
places, including the remote past and the future. The principle of induction,
a conclusion from "many" to "all," can never be cited as proof for the vera-
city of the conclusions drawn from it. It is the faith in the order and continuity of nature which we experience and to which there are no exceptions
(on this point see further below). But on the basis of this principle we make
predictions upon which we stake, if necessary, considerable financial invest-
ments. In recent times, where physical laws were based on statistical laws,
the difficulty of this philosophical problem has not been eased. The foundation of statistics is the law of big numbers. It has no basis in actual experience.
Why should a dice be "forbidden" to fall one hundred times in a row onto
a six, when the probability to do so is one-sixth at the second and any
subsequent throw, as it was at the first throw? And why should such an
event occur in the "long run" if we have never known a lucky man who
succeeded? But on the basis of these "unproven" laws we are able to send
satellites to the moon, Venus, Mars, Jupiter and achieve tracking and landing
accuracies of fantastic proportions (see W. G. Melhouse, "Navigation between the Planets," *Scientific American*, Vol. 234, No. 6, June 1976).

The success in the outcome of predictions based on the principle of induction is in reality the definition of scientific truth. The stress is laid on the
condition that there be *no* exceptions. Every newly-discovered fact that falls
in line with the assumption strengthens it. The measure of confidence in-

creases with the number of successful applications. This is part of the principle of induction.

It might be useful to point out the characteristic difference between natural science and the science of mathematics. In natural science, the principle of induction is strengthened by each case of successful application, but falls with a single exception. Not so with the principle of induction in mathematics, which can be proven as a consequence of the axioms of algebra. The principle assures us that, under specific conditions, if a statement is true for a given number $m$, then it is true for all numbers $n$, no matter how large, as long as they are finite. Even if the number $n$ is so large that it would defy even the capacity of a large computer, we would not have to rely on good faith to believe, that that which has been formulated on the basis of the principle of induction, and is true for $m$, is true for $n$ as well.

### Systematics as a source of insight into Ma'aseh Bereshith

The problem discussed in connection with the applicability of mathematics to the physical world appears also in connection with systematics, another tool of inquiry into the real world. We formulate systems into which we classify natural objects, be they minerals or rocks, plants or animals, or even stars. We are convinced that this classification expresses some actual order amongst the things created. To classify an object correctly is not just a verbal debate, but the explanation of a fact and characteristic of the given object. We are confident that the system of classification, which is the brain-child of man, has a counterpart in the real world. The Lord created this order with classes and species. Discoveries of details of this classification which parallel our abstract systems thus reveal to us details of *Ma'aseh Bereshith*.

### Objection to the use of the principle of induction and systematics

Objections against the principle of induction are based mainly on its extension into the unknown past. If we knew that at a given moment in the past the conditions in the universe were different from those at present, it would be obvious that the principle cannot be applied. At the creation, the creative word of God was decisive and influenced all processes until the conclusion of the sixth day.

Furthermore, since we have evidence of the dynamic nature of the universe and have no conclusive evidence for a steady rate of change, all conclusions drawn from the application of the principle of induction to the distant past are not reliable. How then can those facts that seemingly point to a longer extension to the application of the principle of induction be explained? Two explanations are proposed.

1)   The time schedule at creation, measured on our present schedule of 24 hours per day, was much more condensed. Events that take a day took a fraction of a second at the time of creation. Thus, at the time scale of creation, an animal whose fossil we find imbedded in a layer of sedimentary rock was born, grew, died, and became a fossil almost instantaneously on our present time scale. What seems to us to have needed thousands of years was condensed into a few seconds of creation time.

One objection against this argument is that it encompasses only a change of words. It would be analagous to the midrashic explanation that a day of the Creator is equivalent to a thousand years on the human scale.

A more serious objection stems from the fact that at an accelerated time, all laws of nature become void. For instance, the acceleration due to gravity on earth is approximately 10m/sec/sec. At an accelerated time scale, something on earth must have fallen much more slowly, unless the mass of the earth was increased by the time scale factor, which possibly would have given it the mass of a "black hole". Of course, one could object that the laws of nature were not created with nature, but were instituted suddenly at the end of the creation time scale. Too many facts would then become inexplicable. "If it were not for my covenant, the laws of heaven and earth I would not have instituted" (*Jeremiah* 33:25, 26).

2)   Facts that seem to point to a long time-span are fictive only. Layers of sedimentary rocks, one upon the other, do not mean that one is older than the other. If fossils are found in them, that does not mean that they were once living animals and became fossilized. The world we observe today with all its fantastic detail was created just as it is, as a "fully developed" world. If these details fall well in line with the application of the principle of induction, then, the argument continues, God created the world "as if" a time sequence prevailed, though everything was created more or less instantaneously.

This argument too is only a semantic one. If the world was created "as if," then the principle of induction is applicable, and scientists can argue which layer is older, how much older, etc. But there is a more serious objection! If God endowed man with an inquisitive mind that forces him to recognize a time sequence in the observed facts of creation, He would have created this world with the intention of misleading man (Heaven forbid), whom He created as the crown of His creation, in His own image.

Eliezer Berkowitz defined this viewpoint in a penetrating article, ("Scientific and religious world view," *AOJS Intercom*, Jan. 1965): "It is the very nature of the human being — who is the subject of perception of nature — that recognizes order, law, unity, and continuity. To program, define and discover the realization of planned intentions, are characteristics of human existence. At the same time they apply to the innermost reality of the world of objects . . . This is not just an abstract idea . . . It is one of the basic conditions, on which depends the possibility of existence of an object . . . the relationship between the existence of the object, and existence of the subject had to be found in the common world of both: the will of the Creator in a creation which has an intent of purpose right from the beginning."

It would be difficult to conceive such a purpose in an intent to mislead man. Any alternative is preferable. If the midrashic sources allow for an extension of time back to creation, this alternative is not only preferable but nearly unavoidable.

## Geology and the age of the world

Geologists and paleontologists are accused of intentionally extending the age of the universe to rescue the theory of evolution which, as a process of gradual change by chance mutation, requires a nearly infinite time period. Nothing would be more wrong than to believe that a longer age of the universe had to be assumed only for the sake of the theory of evolution. I want to show by a few examples why Wuerzburger, in the quotation at the beginning of this article, "has no doubt, whatsoever, that there is no possibility to explain the existence of the world within a duration of only 5728 years".

1) Systematics and classification are legitimate tools of the scientific exploration of *Ma'aseh Bereshith*. Petrology classifies the rocks into two main classes: Igneous rocks and sedimentary rocks. The two names are unfortunate for the present discussion, as they are not descriptive but explanatory; hence already picture a theory. But the division is obvious to any alert observer. On the one hand, we have rocks which consist exclusively of crystalline minerals randomly distributed within the body of the rock. On the other hand, we find rocks which consist nearly exclusively of one type of mineral, either aluminum hydrosilicates (clay minerals), or carbonates (lime, dolomite), or quartz, "sand". These sand kernels show signs of wear and tear of transportation on their surface. Neither clay minerals nor carbonate

minerals occur in the other group. The second group appears exclusively in layers, while the former group does not generally show such layering. Laboratory experiments and field experience near volcanoes show that such rocks with a crystalline texture form when molten rock material (magma) solidified by cooling. Hence the name: igneous rock, derived from hot fiery rock-melt.

If not exposed at the surface, crystalline igneous rocks are found everywhere underneath the cover of sedimentary rocks. Where the drill penetrates deeply, it pierces crystalline rocks. Where no such evidence is available, seismic records show their presence underneath. The existence of these sedimentary rock layers on top of the crystalline basement can be explained only by time-consuming processes. Clay minerals and carbonate minerals form by weathering of silicate minerals of igneous rocks or by secondary weathering of sedimentary rocks. The geological record shows such sedimentary layers in great numbers, in some locations to a total thickness of 20 to 30 km. To produce just the quantity of sedimentary rock minerals by weathering would take much longer than a few thousand years, exclusive of their settling down to form layers upon layers — layers that subsequently were deformed, folded, upturned, eroded, levelled and again covered with new layers of sediments (unconformities). Such processes take a long time. Motion along known active faults are of the order of a few millimeters a year, or, in sudden catastrophic events (California earthquake 1906), several centimeters. But we have evidence of several hundred and even thousand meters of dislocation. Moreover, every layer bears evidence of life that existed during its formation including animals and plants which lived their life cycle from birth to death and were buried within the accumulating sediments and are preserved as fossils, a process which requires displacement, molecule by molecule, of the inorganic (or sometimes even the organic) material by mineralic material, processes which require time.

Then there are the sandstones of which each grain appears microscopically to be either highly polished (like having passed through a polishing machine) or frosted (as seen in artificial sand blasting); sometimes pitted or scratched or rounded or subrounded, but rarely with original crystal surfaces. All these wonderful details speak of processes that required eons of time.

2)  From such details geologists have been able to reconstruct conditions and processes which might have prevailed at the time of the formation of the particular layer of rock. On the basis of such conclusions, they can predict where mineral resources can be found or where the drill should be set to look

for oil in the deeper layers of the earth. Whenever oil is found, it is associated with salt water in the pore space of the oil-carrying rock. In order to accumulate enough oil in one location to facilitate withdrawal by pumping, the carrier rock must be tilted, so that the oil can rise by gravitation to the upper part of the formation. To discover such conditions, hidden from direct observation by hundreds and thousands of meters of overlying sedimentary rocks, all kinds of geophysical prospecting methods are employed. In addition, events from the past must be discovered which "trapped" the oil and allowed accumulation in the high spot of the formation, either faulting, folding, unconformities, or change in rock porosity. All these items point to events which require long time periods. It is this corroboration between theoretical considerations and technological realities which carries verification with it, as well as the *raison d'être* of geological investigation. Hence, the quotation cited at the beginning of this paper.

3) Some minerals of igneous rocks, especially magnetite, become magnetized by the prevailing earth's magnetic field when the rock is cooled below a certain temperature (Curie point, about 470°C). In sedimentary rock, such remnant magnetization can also be found. While magnetic grains settle, they orient themselves in the direction of the earth's magnetic field. Apparently paradoxically, it has been found that some rocks are magnetized in a direction opposite to that of the present magnetic field of the earth. Geophysicists have been able to show a remarkable sequence of field reversals in igneous rocks of various ages. With the advent of air-towed and ship-towed magnetometers, a remarkable discovery was made in the early 1960's in the Pacific Ocean off the west coast of the United States. The sea floor showed a pattern of north-south oriented stripes of positive and negative magnetization. Subsequently a similar system, symmetrically located on both sides of the mid-Atlantic ridge south of Iceland, was discovered. An explanation of this striping can be found by assuming that the volcanic rocks of the mid-Atlantic ridge are of different ages and passed through the Curie point at times when the magnetic field of the earth was oriented in opposite and reversed direction. The width and the sequence of the stripes correspond to the adequately dated reversals in volcanic rocks mentioned earlier. The same sequence of remnant magnetization has been found in marine sediments recovered in deep-sea cores by the American exploratory global marine expedition of the Glomar Challenger (*Geotimes* 1971–1973). The independent appearance of the same sequence and relative time schedule of magnetic reversals speaks of the reality of these surprising geophysical measurements.

Though they cover only recent geological events, their time schedule cannot be covered by only a few thousand years.

### The fossil record and the theory of evolution

As previously shown, if we accept fossil records as real and not fictive, we must assume that life on earth did not appear all at once, say in the time span of a few days. Proponents of the theory of evolution use fossil evidence to hypothesize that plants and animals of all kinds of phyla developed through mutations from each other, and that higher forms of life developed from lower forms, and the latter from one-celled life forms.

Numerous and serious objections have been raised against the validity of this theory. One group of objectors shows that the assumptions of the theory are wrong and cannot be proven. This type of argumentation is summarized by Y. R. Etzion in *Hamayan* (Vol. 8, Nos. 1–3), by Lee N. Spetner ("A new look at the theory of evolution," *Proceed. AOJS*, vol. 1; reprinted in *Challenge*, p. 198) and by Morris Goldman ("A critical review of evolution," *Challenge*, p. 216).

The other group of arguments against the theory of evolution shows that no form of life, even the most primitive, could have come about by mere chance. Mathematicians have shown that the probability that a single molecule of protein or a gene or a single living cell occurred by random mixture of molecules is so fantastically small as to be impossible. (See for instance E.H. Simon, "On gene creation," *Proceed. AOJS*, vol. 1, reprinted in *Challenge*, p. 208). Even granted any length of time, statistical laws never *confirm* that events of such small probabilities occur. G. N. Schlesinger ("The empirical basis of belief in God," *Challenge*, footnote, p. 410) claims that any possible event, no matter how rare, is bound to occur somewhere and at some times, given infinite time and space.

The "positing of a self-directed upward-pointing arrow of ever more complex organisms," as Harry Faier aptly termed it (*Intercom*, Vol. XII, No. 2), is another factual difficulty. The "upward arching arrow" is an expression of the increase in dissymmetry, which is impossible to achieve by chance. Lecomte du Nouy (*Human Destiny*, Longmans, Green & Co., N.Y. 1947) explains the meaning of dissymmetry by the example of 500 grains of white powder stacked in a narrow tube upon 500 grains of black powder. When the tube is turned upside down the powder empties into a spherical glass bowl. After a little more shaking the powder appears grey. This is dissymmetry. No matter how many times the powder is poured back into the tube, or how many times the bowl is shaken, a complete separation of the grains into a white and black column in the tube can never be achieved except by a miracle. The mathematics of probability expresses such a miracle by a low probability of the order $10_{-n}$, where n is a large number. Organic molecules are of the type of a high dissymmetry. It would be impossible to achieve it by chance mixing.

The second law of thermodynamics states that in an isolated material system each successive state entails a definite decrease in energy. Not only can we not expect the formation of a dissymmetry as the starting point of life, but physical laws forbid the increase in dissymmetry or even its continuation. Each successive state tends to a lower energy level. Life, on the other hand, has the tendency to increase the level of energy from the lower forms to higher forms. This is an insurmountable obstacle for an "upward arching arrow" towards more complex forms of life by nothing else but chance.

All living things exhibit the distinctive characteristic of design. Even a single cell is differentiated in such a fashion that each part is designed to perform a special task, not to speak of any part of a more complex entity of a living organism, a leaf of a tree, the wing of a bird, the eye of an animal. To deny a design is tantamount to denying the existence of these objects. You have only to look at the design on the wing of a butterfly to be convinced that it is utterly impossible to conceive it as a chance happening; you will be unable to understand its existence without admitting design.

When we finally consider the brain of man, who himself is able to design, who himself is able to think purposefully, who amongst many other things was able to invent statistics and mathematics, then "scientists who spend their life with the purpose of proving that it is purposeless constitute an interesting subject of study" (Whitehead, quoted in *Human Destiny*, p. 43).

### Design in Ma'aseh Bereshith

If life on earth is an "upward arching arrow", the whole creation must have been designed to make such an upward trend possible. Among the one-hundred-odd chemical elements, the four essential to organic chemistry, H, C, N, O, are from the lower end of the periodic table of elements, and hence are of low atomic weight (H–1, C–12, N–14, O–16). Their unique atomic structure facilitates the formation of multiple-linked rings, long chains, and complicated helices, so characteristic of organic molecules.

## Water, the liquid of special design

Of these four elements two, H and O, form water, $H_2O$, the bulk material of the organic cell. Its molecules have a unique property. They are electrically not neutral but have positive and negative electric charges on opposite sides of the molecule, that is to say, they are polar (Fig. 1). Water is the solvent of most chemical elements and compounds. It is the life-giving fluid that is able to transport nutrients to the cells of organic bodies, to remove waste

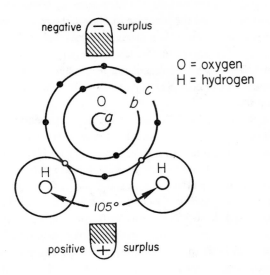

## Fig. I. POLARITY OF $H_2O$ MOLECULE

FIGURE 1 illustrates the notion of polarity of the water molecule.

(a)  nucleus of oxygen atom with 8 positive charges (protons).

(.)  8 electrons of the O atom, two at the inner, higher energy level (b), and 6 at the outer, lower energy level (c).

(0)  Unfilled electron positions at ring (c), occupied now by the two single electrons of two H atoms. These two electrons are now jointly shared by the O atom and the H atom. Though the compound $H_2O$ has combined an equal number of protons and electrons, and so is, as a whole, electrically neutral, its charges are not equally distributed within the molelcule. The originally neutral O atom has now $1/2 \cdot (1+1) = 1$ electron charge more than previously, while the originally neutral two H atoms have now correspondingly 1 electron charge less. Hence the side of the molecule where the two H atoms are located has a surplus of positive charge, the opposite side a surplus of negative charge. Thus the molecule has definite electric polarity.

products, to dissolve inorganic matter and to convey the solution to the roots of plants. In addition to this marvellous design is the fact that only on earth — the life-supporting planet — does water exist in sufficient quantities to sustain life. Water occurs naturally in the solid, the liquid, and vapor states. It covers more than 70 % of the earth's surface as oceans, at an average depth of 5 km.

Due to its polarity, water is able to cling with adhesive force to nearly all surfaces (unless the latter are made water-repellent). Water wets the surfaces of the grains surrounding the pore space of oil-carrying rocks. This allows the oil droplets to float, freely suspended, in the center of each pore space, and these, under pressure, gravitational or artificial, can migrate from pore to pore either to form concentrated oil pools at the top of a "trapped" formation, or move to the low-pressure zone, caused by the pump at the oil well. One must wonder, after recognizing these far-reaching consequences of the polarity of water molecules, whether the one proton and one electron that met "by chance" to enter their monogamous marriage to form an atom of hydrogen, later, out of *Gemiluth Chesed*, satisfied the yearning of the lone oxygen atom to fill in the "painfully" missed two electrons in its outer orbit to form the lopsided water molecule! Did they know at the time what great design they had hit upon "by chance"?

**"A boundary was set which they cannot transgress"** (Psalms, 104:9)

The earth is unique also in that it has not only large quantities of water, but also ocean basins in which these waters collect. How did the Creator divide the waters from the dry land? The crust of the earth has two elevation levels, one the continental level, 75 % of which is below 800 m elevation, and the other, the deep oceanic level, 85 % of which is between –2500 m and –5000 m. Water depths between sea level and –2500 m are found in only 4 % of the surface of the earth. Thus, land and ocean areas are sharply separated with regard to their elevation. The statistician expresses this by stating that the distribution of elevations on earth is bimodal, one maximum being at 700 m elevation, the other at 4400 m below sea level.

By which grand design is this surprising bimodality achieved? It was discovered (1904) through seismic records that, at a depth of approximately 35 km under continental areas, the seismic wave velocity suddenly increases, compared to the velocity in the rocks above that depth. The seismic velocity in the upper 35 km corresponds to a velocity in rocks with high silica and aluminum (SIAL) content, whereas the velocity below 35 km corresponds

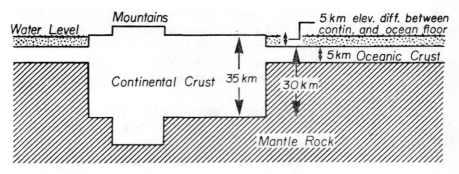

## Fig.2.  ISOSTASY

FIGURE 2 illustrates the concept of isostasy = equal balance of the weight of continental areas against the depressed oceanic area (elevation difference approximately 5 km.). This balance is maintained, according to Archimedes' principle, by displacement of heavier mantle rock (spec. grav. approx. 3.2) by lighter rocks of the continental crust (spec. grav. approx. 2.8). Thickness of continental crust approx. 35 km., displaced mantle rock approx. 30 km. (Balance: 35×2.8 approx. 30×3.2). Thus the continents "swim" (according to Archimedes' principle) in the heavier substratum of the mantle, while their tops are buoyed up 5 km. above the level of the oceanic crust. The oceanic depression is filled by the ocean.

to the velocity in rocks with a higher iron-magnesium content (Femic). The former (crust) has a lower specific density than the latter (mantle). The oceanic crust differs from the continental crust in two respects. Its thickness is only 5 km and its density is halfway between that of the continental crust material and that of the mantle. A column of 35 km of continental crust, consisting of lighter rock material, is counterbalanced by a column of 30 km of the heavier rock material (see Fig. 2) in the oceanic area. The higher level of the continents (approximately 5 km above the deep-sea floor) is thus the result of gravitational balance between areas of lighter rocks and heavier rocks. (In fact, below high mountain areas, like the Rockies, the crust-mantle boundary lies much deeper, at about 50 km). No such distinct distribution of light rocks and heavy rocks has been discovered by the space-crafts so far on other planets. It is unique for the earth, the abode of man, to form a bed for the oceans.

### Carbon dioxide in the atmosphere

From the carbon dioxide in the air, plants manufacture carbohydrates for the plant cells, in turn food for animals and man, through the process of photosynthesis (another miracle). The concentration of carbon dioxide ($CO_2$) in air is 0.04% of the atmospheric gases. A higher concentration is detrimental for life as we know it. How did this delicate balance come about, and how is it maintained? The overwhelmingly greater part of $CO_2$ found on earth is chemically bound in carbonate rocks, products of the process of weathering. If there would have been more calcium and magnesium available, all of the available $CO_2$ would have been used up. In the decay of organic matter, in the burning of organic fuel, as well as in volcanic eruptions, $CO_2$ is produced. A delicate balance must, therefore, be maintained if life on earth is to be sustained. Here again water, concentrated in the great oceans, enters the picture. Though $CO_2$ represents only 0.04% of the atmospheric gases, its concentration among the atmospheric gases dissolved in water is much higher. In fact, the amount of $CO_2$ dissolved in the sea in 25 times the entire amount of $CO_2$ in the air. Small changes in the partial pressure of $CO_2$ in the air immediately cause a correspondingly large amount of absorption or release of $CO_2$ from the ocean reservoir. Thus, a splendid regulator was designed into the ocean, which, in turn, is a consequence of the unique design of the polar water molecule.

*"I shall give the rain of your land at the right time"* (Deut. 11:14) — Few realize that the weather pattern on earth depends on the establishment of day and night, i.e., the rotation of the earth about its axis. As a result of this rotation, everything that moves freely on this earth moves in a direction perpendicular to the direction of the pressure differences. Wind, however, when blowing perpendicular to the direction of the pressure differences, is not further accelerated by that force and has reached its upper limit of velocity. In other words, even if the pressure difference is permanent, as for instance between the high-pressure area at the poles and the low-pressure area at the equator, the winds caused by them can reach only an upper limit of velocity. Without this deflecting force of earth's rotation (Coriolis force), winds would blow only north-south, and at velocities such that nothing could exist above the immediate surface of the ground. Life could not exist. Thus, rain in its proper time is a direct consequence of the rotation of the earth, and the deflecting force caused by it.

## Summary

God has not revealed the details of how He created this world. But He has endowed man with the faculty to investigate and discover "the laws of heaven and earth" which He established for the sake of "His covenant" (Jeremiah 33:25). Such investigation negates the thesis of those who attempt to deny a design in this creation, and reveals some of the "miracles and wonders which are with us every day" to sustain life on earth, including man, the crown of *Ma'aseh Bereshith*.

## REFERENCES

*Hamayan*, Vol. 8, Nos. 1 to 4, 5728.

*Challenge*, Torah Views on Science and Its Problems. AOJS of Great Britain,   Feldheim Publishers, N.Y., 1976

Rambam, *Moreh Nevuchim*

Ramban, *Commentary on the Torah*, Mossad Harav Kook, 5719

Ralbag, *Sefer Milchamoth Hashem*

Schwab, Simon, "How old is the universe?" in *Challenge, op. cit.*

Mandelbaum, Hugo, "Torah, facts, and conclusions," Proceed. AOJS, Vol. 1, 1966.

Welhouse, W.G., "Navigation between the planets," *Scientific American*, Vol. 234, No. 6, June 1976.

Thorne, K.S., "The search for black holes," *Scientific American*, Vol. 231, No. 6, Dec. 1974.

Penrose, Roger, "Black holes," *Scientific American*, May 1972.

Berkowitz, Eliezer, "Scientific and religious world views," AOJS, *Intercom*, Jan, 1965.

Spetner, L.N., "A new look at the theory of evolution." Proceed. AOJS, Vol. 1, reprinted in *Challenge, op. cit.*

Goldman, Morris, "A critical view of evolution," *Challenge, op. cit.*

Simon, E.H., "On gene generation," Proceed. AOJS, Vol. 1, reprinted and revised in *Challenge, op. cit.*

Schlesinger, G.N., "The empirical basis of belief in God," *Challenge, op. cit.*

Lecomte de Nouy, *Human Destiny*, Longmans, Green and Co., N.Y., 1947.

*Geotimes*, 1971, 1972, 1973.

# PERSPECTIVE ON THE YETZER HARA: A RE-INTERPRETATION OF TALMUDIC INSTINCTIVISM

Moshe HaLevi Spero

## Introduction

Although the topic of human nature, in general, is an enormous one in both traditional as well as contemporary Jewish thought, I am most specifically interested in an understanding of the role of the *yetzer hara* (herein: *yh*) in relation to a Jewish view of man's nature. Is this *yh* construed as so entrenched in man's being and behavior that one should speak of an intrinsically evil aspect of human nature? Is the *yh* as intrinsic to man as his so-called good nature? This is the opinion of some of the rabbis of the Talmud. By way of generalization, the Talmudic view of the experiment of human life appears to be not so much an exercise in *reason* — as Greek intellectualism assumed — but rather an interaction of opposing tendencies of good and evil implanted in man, and in the subjugation of evil through struggle and effort. It has been asserted that from the historical viewpoint: "Perhaps the most characteristic development which the Pharisaic rabbis made . . . as to the nature of man was in the doctrine of the two *yetzarim*, or inclinations."[1] At the same time, there was never any question of a Manichean dualism implied by this conceptualization. The rabbis were perhaps painfully aware of copious examples of moral corruption in human nature which they explained by the presence in every man of a *yetzer* for evil; much the same as Freud was later to postulate the *death instinct* in reaction to the atrocities of the world war and to other contemporary examples of man's malignant aggressiveness and evil. Yet, the question here is whether or not it is correct

*Rabbi Moshe HaLevi Spero (MSSW — Case Western Reserve Univ.) is a child psychotherapist who has published over two dozen articles on applied and clinical psychotherapy and psychiatry. His articles have also appeared in* Tradition *and* Judaism. *Spero's most recent publication in this field is* " 'Psychiatric Hazard' and the Halachic Disposition Towards Contraception and Abortion," *which appeared in the* Journal of Jewish Communal Service, *(1976). Rabbi Spero is Associate Editor of the* Journal of Psychology and Judaism.

to view this talmudic *yetzer* as a "bad *impulse*, an *agent* . . . whose business it is to lead man astray . . . a natural *impulse* which generally leads man to evil."[2] On the other hand, if the *yh* is not viewed as some instinct, as I will contend, then what is the function of *yh*: in what sense does it "incline" man and just how "evil" and "natural" is man's evil nature?

I will enter this topic by making certain comparisons between the Freudian concepts of human nature — the id, libido, Thanatos (the death instinct) — and the *yetzer hara*. There is a multifold purpose for selecting an entry point so seemingly narrow in scope. On the one hand, we are engaged in scholarly pursuit of a tenable description of the *yh* in modern terminology. For this purpose alone, I would not deal with the principles of Freudianism. However, other authors, while occupied with the same pursuit, have adopted superficial approaches by attempting to establish similarities between the *yh*, the id, and Thanatos on very dubious grounds.[3] Some authors have even attempted to prove that Freud, in formulating his opinions, borrowed, however unacknowledged, from Talmudic and later mystic views on human nature.[4] These Freudian concepts, therefore, become necessary to our discussion.

It will also be of great interest to examine whether or not the rabbis, in their conceptualization of this "evil inclination" in man, fell victim to a totally instinctivist approach, as opposed to an approach more tolerant and cognizant of the so-called "conflict-free ego" or social factors involved in personality development. While it appears *prima facie* that the Talmud, and certainly the overall philosophy of Judaism, is of the opinion that there is an inherent "goodness" to man's nature and that man is qualitatively different from animal[5] — which would surely evince skepticism of radical behaviorism — such a view might not have fostered an awareness of the faults of radical instinctivism. The belief in a uniquely *human* nature may have bound the rabbis to a concomitant belief in distinctly human "evil" or "good" instincts indigenous to that nature.[6]

## II

A brief overview indicating the complexity of this philosophical problem of human nature might be of interest. Many modern psychological frameworks consistently eschew reference to qualities or hypothetical variables said to comprise that vague construct known as human nature. Such positions view the mere description of groups and types of behavior as sufficient for the understanding of man.[7] Skinner, who clearly exemplifies this view, maintains that, "A self or personality is at best a repertoire of behavior imparted by an organized set of contingencies."[8] In defending behaviorism against the very claim that it ignores man *qua* man and assigns no role to the study of human nature, Skinner asserts that he does not deny the existence of human nature but merely adds that it can be amply explained in terms of behavioral contingencies.

> "What is usually meant in saying that behaviorism dehumanizes man is that it neglects important capacities which are not to be found in machines or animals, such as the capacity to choose, have purposes, and behave creatively. But the behavior from which we infer choice and creativity is also *within* the reach of behavioral analysis and it is not clear that it is wholly out of reach of other species. Man is perhaps unique in being a moral animal, but not in the sense that he possesses morality; he has constructed a social environment in which he behaves with respect to himself and others in moral ways."[9]

In other words, Skinner's view is that behaviorism does not *reduce* man or human nature to behavioral responses; he simply argues that human nature has always been nothing more than the sum total of man's behavioral responses. Strangely, however, in its terms, behaviorism has yet to amply explain innate creativity or the intuitive and universal striving for moral and ethical regulation.

Despite this prevalent tendency, it has remained difficult to deny the usefulness of and interest in a concept like human nature, i.e., what is it that makes man *man*? The behaviorist response to this question points to an essential paradox in its world-view. Certainly the behaviorists are not totally incorrect in asserting that the human biological tendency to seek tension reduction or reinforcement is only different in degree from an animal's similar tendencies. On the other hand, when we use the term human nature or "natural man" we wish to connote *that which has not been changed or affected by human action or social demands and expectations.* In this sense, precisely for the behaviorist, natural man is a contradiction because he has become "man" by acts of culture and by changes in the natural state. The concept of human nature which we desire refers to man *prior* to reinforcement schedules and change. In this prior state, behaviorism can only ascribe to "man" *potential* attributes which, in turn, do not entail meaningful descriptive properties about human nature. But they are mistaken because even mere existence, in the existential sense, can be used as a predicate. "Human nature, even in its uncorrupted state . . . is already stamped by consciousness of its own being."[10]

Moreover, I side with the oft-defended argument that even when one views man's entire behavior repertoire as a unit, it is qualitatively different from the purely organismic, instinctive responses demonstrated by lower species of life. "We must not forget that, in contrast to animals, man is a being who not only behaves but also reflects about how he behaves . . . has the ability to question his behavior . . . who faces the question: *after satisfaction, what? . . .* who asks: *Am I needed?*"[11] Thus, the need to retain the concept of a specifically human nature emerges as a defensible and meaningful one for inquiries such as ours which concern man's understanding of his uniquenesses — regardless of whether or not certain superficial principles of behavior formation apply to both man and animal alike.

In talking of man's nature, however, past philosophers and psychologists have also attempted to refer to an overall quality of this nature's "personality," viz., good, evil, or neither. Whatever the description, there has always had to be some source for the particular value judgment posited as being the correct one. If, for example, man's *nature* is inherently evil, some role or status is thereby given to the unconscious motivating forces, drives or contingencies which seem to impinge upon and color this personality. Are these very forces themselves considered intrinsic or extrinsic to a human's being? Does one say that if man has an "evil drive," then he has an "evil nature" as well? Or, if man has an "evil nature," must he therefore have "evil drives"? Is the force which determines man's nature as much a part of that nature as the end result of that force? These are important questions, inasmuch as philosophers usually view the end results when labeling the cause!

The answer, in part, depends upon one's orientation. For proponents of the traditional instinct theories — orthodox psychoanalysis, H. Marcuse, K. Menninger, for example — those instincts which contribute to man's basic sensuality or aggressiveness are understood as making man "sensual" or "aggressive" *by nature* and are *part of* his sensuous and aggressive nature. On the other hand, those claiming that social reinforcement alone produces man's aggressiveness — such as the behaviorists — are of the opinion that (a) no instinctive, natural predisposition is the necessary or sufficient source of this trait; therefore, (b) the aggressiveness is not an indigenous part of man's nature, and (c) we should cease all talk about man's aggressive "nature."

Historically, the instinctivists were correct in that they at least grappled with the problem of what makes man unique. Since the radical instinct theories are largely discredited, there has been little resultant validation of a non-instinctivist approach to human nature. "The problem of the image of man, instead of being clarified, was evaded."[12] One good reason is that when the 1920's witnessed the fall of instinctivism, the latter was not ousted by "another theory concerning a similar domain of behavior," but rather by a "different approach to social psychology."[13] This new approach was actually a narrowing of the scope of psychology, away from the general, synthetic questions to more narrow issues — those of empirical researchability. Skinner's psychology, and certainly that of the earlier radical behaviorists, were direct outcomes of this situation. The behaviorists' error has been in equating man's essence with his manifestations. The search for a general explanation of human being encompassing human nature was, for the most part, abandoned.[14]

### III

Initial reference to the *yetzer hara* is encountered in a Biblical passage in which God says, "*For I know the yetzer of man.*"[15] Schechter correctly indicates that *yetzer* can be understood to simply mean *imagination* or *desire* whatever the nature of that desire: good or bad.[16] However, other Biblical passages attribute a specific character to this *yetzer*; viz., "*the* yetzer *of the heart of man is evil even from his youthful days,*"[17] and "*he understands all the imaginations of the thoughts (kol yetzer machshavot),*" where *yetzer* is said to mean two hearts and two *yetzarim* (plural); the "bad heart" with its bad *yetzer* and the "good heart" with its good *yetzer*.[18] In another tradition, the rabbis explicate the extra letter *yud* in the word *vayyitzer* (in the passage, *Then the Lord formed* [vayyitzer] *the man of dust . . .*)[19] as a hint to a belief in two types of *yetzer*: good and evil.[20]

We thus begin to see some conception of two forces in man, one of which is called *ra*; literally translated, evil. We shall see, however, that *ra* is a word whose connotations can mean something other than evil. In general, one finds this *yetzer hara* to be the more conspicuous of the two *yetzarim* throughout the later sources. Several opinions found in Midrashic and Talmudic literature add to the picture of an evil, scheming "enemy" or drive in man. Some rabbis stated, ". . . the *yetzer hara* is problemsome in that [even] man's [basic] nature is called evil, as it is written, *for the nature of man's heart is evil from his youth.*"[21] Or, "Two *yetzarim* were created by the

Holy One ... a *yetzer* for idolatry and a *yetzer* for licentiousness. The former has already been destroyed while the latter still persists."[22] Another observation reads, "Come and see [what is the case] with the goat or kid; once it sees a deep pit it retreats since there is no *yh* in an animal. Yet, the human infant is made headstrong by the *yh*; he carelessly touches a snake or scorpion."[23] Finally, "The good *yetzer* is poor and weak and has nothing to show as a reward for obedience to it. The evil *yetzer* is strong. Whatever the former is able to acquire through tireless labor, the latter snatches away easily by holding forth the immediate rewards of wordly pleasure."[24]

I have carefully refrained from over-use of the phrases "evil *impulse*" or "evil *instinct*" which are usually acceptable translations for *yetzer hara*, because there is yet to be discussed evidence which indicates that *yh* might not denote evil *per se* in an ethically judgmental sense. Furthermore, it is not at all clear that a *yh* is similar to what psychoanalysis lables "instinct" or really was conceived of as an "impulse" in human nature. I shall now examine both issues in turn.

## IV

The first qualification has already been observed by scholars, based upon the following types of evidence from the Talmud: "There is no evil inclination that does not contain a thread of the holy inclination."[25] Rabbi Samuel b. Nathan stated: "*And behold it was good* is a reference to the good *yetzer*, while *behold it was very good*[26] is a reference to the evil *yetzer*. But is the evil *yetzer* to be considered very good? Actually, yes, for without the evil *yetzer* man would not marry, build a house, beget children or engage in business."[27] Based on this, one writer concludes, "Even the *yh* which corresponds roughly to man's untamed natural (and especially sexual) appetites or passions, is not intrinsically evil, and, therefore, should not be completely repressed."[28] Similarly, concludes Solomon, "the evil *yetzer*, as manifested socially and unmodified by the good *yetzer*, is considered in Jewish tradition to be 'evil.' However, intrapsychically, it has neutral moral value."[29] In other words, since "evil" is a term whose meaning may vary cross-culturally, the particular underlying force which may incline a person toward the fulfillment of basic primary needs (eating, sleeping, procreation, domination, etc.) cannot, *itself*, be rightly called "evil." The fact that the *yetzer hara* causes sin and, as a result — from the rabbinic viewpoint — death,[30] should not make it an *evil yetzer* but, at most, a *yetzer* to do acts which are sometimes considered evil and/or deviant.

From this observation, various conclusions are possible. One is that if the *yh* represents a neutral life-force it could possibly be seen as an analogue to Freud's concept of libido. Indeed, Solomon suggests that "... the evil inclination ... may be seen, actually, as the psychic energy, libido."[31] Moreover, if the *yh* seems to cause behavior by its obedience to some sort of pleasure principle, then again, perhaps it represents the more primitive part of the psyche, the id, which also operates by such a principle.

On the other hand, the Talmudic view of the *yh* as a cause of death, destruction, regression and aggression bears a closer resemblance to Thanatos.[32] If it is true that the *yh* causes man to "return to earth" and to have backslidings in his personality development, is this not distinctly similar to Freud's own statement concerning the death instinct, to wit: "We may suppose that the final aim of the destructive instinct is to reduce living things to an inorganic state. For this reason we call it a death instinct."[33]

Solomon comes close to dealing with the last possibility but veers off course and, instead, suggests an historical antecedent for Thanatos in an arcane rabbinic view of death *qua* biological cessation of life. "As for Thanatos, there is also a lodging in Jewish tradition ..., in the Torah of R. Meir it was found written, *and it was very good*; and behold *death* is good."[34] The author chooses to explain that tradition as meaning, "... death ... is not the end of life, but a part of the cycle of eternity. It is God's implement for change and rebirth. Without it man would have no incentive for productive work."[35] This view seems to equate Thanatos with death itself rather than with the *yh* or with any impulse towards death.

Freud's view of Thanatos was an entirely pessimistic conception and to this construct he relegated only dysfunctional characteristics; he considered it responsible for man's essential aggressiveness and for often-exhibited self-destructive and self-defeating behaviors.[36] The death instinct expresses an innate tendency towards catabolism, i.e., an organism's fatal evolution towards stagnation and inertia. Furthermore, Freud thought that if the earliest state of an organism was an inanimate one, this regulatory principle of the aggression drive (the death instinct) called for a return to the state of death.

In Freud's view, the above is a portrait of an instinct which is, in fact, the antithesis of constructiveness or of "an incentive for productive work." Thanatos, itself, would tend to draw man away from productivity. Moreover, unlike Eros, the energy of Thanatos cannot even be sublimated into productivity; only true libido can be sublimated. "All man's constructive ability comes from the libido. The only thing which cannot be reduced to Eros is the destructive instinct."[37] It would seem from this discussion that there is no real basis for the concept of Thanatos in R. Meir's view of the possible motivating and growth-provoking capacity of death, *per se*. Thanatos was postulated as a hypothetical intrapsychic variable, an instinct, while the latter — R. Meir's concept — is, at most, a philosophical way to approach death. I will say more about this shortly.

The second issue Solomon discusses — and it is moot for us as well — is whether or not the *yh* can be equated with libido or, in extension, with its locus, the id? The similarity which Solomon feels the *yh* and libido share is that they both seem to represent life-forces which are above value judgment. And it is true, we have seen, that the *yh* cannot be considered an "evil" instinct. However, at this point, we must pause to question whether it was understood as an instinct.

## V

Whether or not the *yh* is an analogue to either the id or Thanatos is an issue which has validity only after one has proven that the *yh* is, in fact, also some type of instinct. Actually, "instinct" is merely the accepted translation for certain entities which Freud called *triebe*. *Trieb* and *instinkt* in German have quite different connotations. "*Instinkt* implies a fixed pattern of response to stimuli — like the web-spinning behavior of a spider. *Triebe*, on the other hand, pertain to stimuli which create a demand for some behavioral response . . . All that Freud insisted upon was the necessity for assuming an internal motivating source, in contrast to the radical empiricists who viewed the organism as merely the passive recipient and recorder of external experiences."[38] Furthermore, Freud's concept of *triebe* implies only an internal excitation which requires discharge. It does not imply fixed, unlearned responses.[39] Thus, some writers have suggested that "drive" would be a more instructive term for *aggressiveness* and *destructiveness*. Yet, as for the constructs of the id and Thanatos, perhaps instinct is still a better description of how Freud viewed them. Simple erotic and destructive tendencies, i.e., drives for particular incidents of the need to perform constructive or destructive acts, seem to be *psychological* concepts derived from clinical observation; the life and death "instincts" — Eros and Thanatos — are *biological* concepts. The latter are not psychic representations of endosomatic stimuli (drives) but are biological trends similar or equal to metabolism and catabolism. *Acts* involving man's essential destructiveness, for example, should be seen as expressions of a destructive drive which, in turn, is seen as a derivative of Thanatos.

Thus, the destructive drives must be seen as *manifestations* of the hypothesized Thanatos. Indeed, "The death instinct itself does not appear as an element of psychological interpretations suggested in [psycho]analysis. Interpretations may refer to destructive or constructive strivings, but their biological root is not relevant for psychological investigation and treatment, just as the assumption made by some theoretical biologists, that the mortality of all living organisms is ultimately due to the principle of entropy, the second theorem of thermodynamics, has no direct bearing upon the study and treatment of cardiac failure."[40]

In Freud's fourth revision of his drive theory, he hypothesized a structural organization for both the life and death instincts which he called the id.[41] That is, both the constructive, sexual drives as well as the destructive, aggressive drives stem from instincts contained in the id. Thus, the id, itself, cannot be called "good" or "bad" as we indicated above. It is a term which always refers to both instincts. If we accept, therefore, that destructiveness and constructiveness are both drives which stem from instincts, Thanatos and Eros, contained in the id, and that Thanatos and Eros are instincts of the sort described, is the *yh* similar either to an instinct or to a drive?

## VI

In the three possible comparisons which could be made between the *yh* and either 1) the entire construct of the id, 2) the death instinct or 3) any specific constructive or destructive drive, there appears insufficient evidence to indicate that the *yh* represents any of these.

First, I question whether the *yh* is an instinct at all. An instinct is some stimulus which arises within the body (endosomatic) which can become conscious only through the ideas and affect which become associated with the expression of its aims.[42] There is simply no direct statement in the Talmud or Midrash that alludes to anything similar to this.[43] The sources do, however, discuss the age at which the *yh* is first supposed to exist in the individual. R. Judah originally felt that the *yh* was already present in the embryonic state, which might have substantiated the argument for an innate, somatic position, but later came to believe that, "At the door [of man's entering the world] the sin lieth."[44] Thus, R. Judah seems to have rejected the "innate" position in favor of one which sees the *yh* as a more post-uterine developmental phenomenon. Other Talmudic sources concur that while the *yetzer tov*, the good inclination, first comes to an individual at the age of thirteen, the *yh* is already present at earliest childhood.[45] This, in fact, is the general consensus of opinion on that matter. It is also true that the *yh* is depicted as having both destructive as well as constructive powers.[46] In this sense, it was viewed as some type of life-force. Yet, to say that it is an instinct is simply false. The past experiences of a child's interactions with his or her parents, for example, are certainly forces in our lives but they are surely not instincts. The *yh* is simply not any kind of biological construct. Thus, we must reject the first hypothesis.

<h2 style="text-align:center">VII</h2>

Does the *yh* represent an antecedent to the death instinct? We have already mentioned the obvious disparity between *views* of death and the death instinct. Let me add that since the *yh* is not an instinct it, therefore, cannot be analagous to Thanatos. Moreover, the general Talmudic view of total human momentum and of the nature of historical change is a forward, teleological and constructive model. The belief in the Messiah, in the After-World and in the ability of man to repent are all indications of the Talmud's particularly progressive, non-catabolistic *weltanschauung*. So, while death, destructiveness and aggressiveness may stem from the *yh*, there is too much contradiction involved in equating the latter with Thanatos.

That the *yh* contains *both* constructive and destructive attributes may lead one to compare it with the id – the id being the locus of both Eros and Thanatos. The difficulty encountered here is that while id drives are un-conscious — "The drives of the id are unconscious not only in a descriptive sense but also in a dynamic sense in that their access to consciousness is actively opposed"[47] — rabbinic sources maintain that one has complete control over the *yh*.[48] Moreover, while superficially both constructs seem to operate on a pleasure principle, in the *yh* this refers simply to the traditional belief that unrestricted hedonic pursuit is primitive, contrary to the Jewish way of life and, thus, evil, while in the id, this principle implies that an organism has a tendency to rid itself of tensions — both external as well as derived from drives — by the most immediate route. The drive for the pur-suit of worldly pleasure by the *yh* is no analogue to Freud's more sophisticated tension-reduction mechanism of the id.

<h2 style="text-align:center">VIII</h2>

Is the belief that the "*yetzer* for licentiousness" still persists as a dominant inclination in man at all similar to that of the pervasiveness of libido *qua* the energy of the sexual drive?[49] Again, there is only a semantic similarity. Sexuality, in psychoanalysis, refers not merely to matters pertaining to copulation or preparatory to it but includes all sensual strivings and satisfactions (competition, need for achievement, need to create, etc.). "Sexuality, in the Freudian sense, does not begin at puberty, after an asexual childhood, nor does it end with the end of genital discharge; it starts at birth or nearly so, and ends with death. Sexuality penetrates most of our activities which are to a large extent, though by no means only, satisfactions of sexual drives."[50] Now, it is again true that some sources indicated that the *yh, probably* including *its* particular sexual connotation, begins at birth or nearly so. This, again, is merely a fortuitous commonality. Libido is seen as a deep-seated force for all constructive activities. In the course of a normal development, libido, or sexual energy becomes cathected to various body organs and undergoes what Freud termed the "vicissitudes of the libido," i.e., the direction of this energy inward, outward, towards fixation, regression or sublimation.[51]

It seems that the sexuality inherent to the *yh*, on the other hand, refers only to sexual offenses or, on the positive level, to the fulfillments of marriage. *There is no indication that the concept of the* yh *encompasses a theory of the eroticization of other organs of the body.* Moreover, we can argue that if someone holds that the *yh* represents destructive forces, then it cannot be libido since libido, as originally postulated by Freud, is unable to explain aggression and narcissism. Furthermore, the drive of the *yh* is never related to any mechanism like sublimation. Sublimation implies that the sexual drive *itself* is manifested and released in the "higher" activities of culture and personality which the sexual need has called into being.[52] Sublimation also connotes Freud's opinion that "higher" psychic activities *as such* are brought into being through sexual activity and are nothing but disguised manifestations of this activity. "The 'higher' activity is a way of escape created by the libido."[53] Once again, while the *yh* is sometimes spoken of as the motivator for specific constructive activities, it is nowhere viewed as *specific energy sublimated into* psychic or life activities, aspirations or cultural perfection. In general, the Talmud could not accept a view which holds that all of life's activities are motivated by extrinsic causes or that they are, in reality, regressions.[54] Even repentence, *t'shuvah* — which literally means "return" — represents creative, forward growth to the Talmudists.[55]

## IX

From the analysis of the meaning and use of the term *yh* and of Freud's psychoanalytic concepts thus far, I would conclude that there can be no comparison between them for the following summarized reasons. The *yh* is not:

1.  An instinct *per se*, because the *yh* is neither an endosomatic construct nor is it a biological one;

2.  Thanatos, because thanatos is an instinct and is purely destructive, regressive and catabolistic, which does not fit into the overall Talmudic world-view;

3.  Eros, because eros is an instinct and does not alone explain destructiveness and aggression;

4.  Libido, because libido is a somatic energy of specific quantity which operates on a tension-reduction principle and through sublimation — concepts not clearly established in rabbinic literature;

5.  The id, because the id is the reservoir of libido, is the housing of both Eros and Thanatos, and is a means of primitive phylogenetic drives which seek expression through various symptoms and sublimated activities which the *yh* does not seem to possess. Finally, the *yh* neither stimulates all life activities nor is it transmogrified into higher cultural or spiritual development.

What then is a proper conceptualization of the *yetzer hara*, bereft as we now seem to be of the instinct approach?

## X

To shed new light on this matter, let me introduce the highly perceptive words of Samson Raphael Hirsch on the subject of the *yetzer hara*. "We have already pointed out that *yetzer* (Genesis 6:5) does not designate an active, impelling force, but the passive result of one, *that which the mind forms, makes the ideal for which it strives* (italics mine — MHS)."[56] The source for this conceptualization originated elsewhere in Hirsch's commentary. In commenting on the passage *And the inclinations of the thoughts of man's heart are but evil all the day*, Hirsch states unequivocally, "It is unfortunate that this word *yetzer* is so often translated as 'instinct,' 'inclination,' or 'impulse' as if it was a force in man that drives him to evil . . . Already in the root [of the word] *yetzer* there is absolutely nothing of forcing, but rather of formation . . . the grammar of the word *yetzer* is not active at all, but passive; it does not mean 'the one who forms' but 'that which is formed.' *Yetzer*, the *idea*, the picture of what we can achieve, certainly does urge, 'tempt' us to achieve it, but *we ourselves have formed it*. If this *idea* be good, then we strive for the good, and also the reverse is true."[57]

What Hirsch is postulating is that the *yh* is neither an internal instinct nor impulse nor is it even a "quasi-external agency", *à la* Schechter. It is simply no agent whatsoever. Man is neither inclined and certainly not compelled to act; rather the *yh* is an after-the-fact description of man's character once man errs and pursues evil ideals. The *yh*, in a very real sense, is man, *himself*, if he chooses to make his ideal and his life-style *ra* or evil. Man's basic nature, in Hirsch's view, is neither evil nor necessarily inclined towards evil.

We can then inquire as to what function is served by man's choosing to make evil, destructiveness and vice his ideals. If man consistently chooses evil, then is there not something leaning man in that direction; something inherently "evil" about his disposition and, perhaps, his nature? Skeptical of behaviorism and unable to appeal to instinctivism, how do we understand the *yh* in relation to a theory of human nature? In view of the strong evidence which casts doubt upon the alleged naturalness of man's aggressiveness and evilness, I suggest that we examine S. R. Hirsch's comments on the *yh* more closely for his more ontologically sound response to the question of why man chooses to have evil ideals.

Man has so-called existential needs that are rooted in his very existence-as-such, over and beyond his basic physiological or even psychological needs. Such needs include relatedness, love, trust, authenticity, creativity, constructivity, identity — to mention but a few of those contributed by the many existentialist philosophers and psychoanalysts.[58] These needs, or character-rooted passions (after Fromm), are the same for all mankind though individual ways of relating to these needs may differ from person to person.[59] Any individual has the *need to cause*, but the external manifestation of that need's fulfillment can be either a "passion to love" or a "passion to destroy," while both are successfully *causative*. Whether man's dominant passion is love or destructiveness depends largely on how one interprets and internalizes individual social circumstances. These circumstances operate in reference to man's biologically given situation and not, as the radical instinctivists had assumed, in reference to a wholly undifferentiated intra-psychic momentum.

It is fruitless to say that man is born with drives of aggression and hate *and* state that this fact alone closes the study of human nature. Rather, it is more instructive to say that man, *as an energy-converting and purposive mechanism*, seeks the maximization of his own being and of his sense of self. "When neutral organisms seeks to expand their self-feeling and to extend their control, they must do so in some way in competition with or at the obvious expense of their fellows. And this makes them seem 'motivated by anti-social desires.' But, in reality, the ontological ground is neutral, not in itself destructive."[60]

Man's passions — or what the rabbis termed man's *yetzarim* — are to be understood in terms of the function they serve for the individual as he or she attempts to make sense out of life and to maintain bearings on one's purpose in life. If one chooses to control and destroy rather than to love and create, this choice formalizes one's *yetzer* — a character-passion, a very nature. In this case, the *yetzer* would be a *yetzer hara*. The human organism needs to seek responses for certain inborn needs. These needs are not to be satisfied only after the physiological needs have had their fill. The existential needs are uniquely intense and demanding precisely because man could not be man without them and *these needs* can henceforth be referred to as being the basic material of human nature.

Here, then, is a theory of human nature. Man wants to be a creator — his own creator — to transform his unfinished state of being into one with some goal and purpose. Each man decides on his own and for himself what behavior style he will choose to follow — his self-consciousness demands it.[61] This was the Talmud's feeling when it recorded the decision of Hillel's school, "Better for man not to have been created; after having been created, let him contemplate his actions."[62] It was also Heidegger's belief when he asked, "Has the *Dasein*, as such, ever freely decided and will it ever be able to decide as to whether to come into existence or not?" That is, man's creativity does not freely flow from his biological given-ness, the rest of his life being a mere unfolding of innate instincts and dispositions modified by a few weak efforts to channel them into productivity. On the contrary, man's true being must be molded by him and, indeed, his very existence-for-being must be created. The ethical and moral provisions of the Torah and Jewish life are expressly designed to be the raw material for that endeavor. "Man can only be understood in terms of his total situation, in terms of the demands he is called upon to answer . . . the chief problem of man is not his nature, but what he does with his nature."[63] Hirsch seems to have been similarly persuaded.

## XI

This approach clearly explains the tension in the Talmudic literature concerning its variegated depictions of the *yh*. The apparent polarity of its positions with regard to it — viewing it as containing both good as well as bad impulses; holding it responsible for creativity as well as destructiveness — needs to be understood unidimensionally. That is, *man's character will vacillate between extremes precisely because this is the dialectical process inherent to man's attempting to make existence meaningful to himself.*[64] Thus, in the classic "situation of temptation," we would not speak of man as being torn between two conflicting desires — good and evil — but rather of being torn between a desire which is an expression of one's character, on the one hand, and a higher obligation which is a truer expression of one's essential self, on the other hand; a conflict between what I feel I need to make of myself and what I *ought* to be. Individuals guided by some religious or philosophical system, have a more difficult time in achieving balance than others guided by other systems and both of the above have an easier time than he who is guided by none. The *yh* is only imposed on human behavior *when* perverted to base levels or when indulged to the point of sin. The vicissitudes of the nature of the *yh* and, in extension, of man's nature *vis-a-vis* the *yh* were already hinted at in the ancient Zohar which states, "There is no *sitra achra* [evil *yetzer*] which does not also contain *sitra d'kiddusha* [holy *yetzer*]."[65] In other words, even if man chooses a *yetzer ra*, this choice still indicates that he is at least attempting to make life meaningful — a good and necessary end — even if the path he chooses is an improper one. A dead person has not even a *yetzer hara*!

## Conclusion

Originally the *yh* seemed to be an independent force which somehow inclines man to act. Closer examination suggests that the *yh* is an individual's own creation and, indeed, could be equated with that individual himself. Man's *basic* nature *per se* is neutrally growth-oriented and 'contains' certain needs which stem from that growth orientation. Once these orientations take on real-life manifestations, one can be a little more descriptive of man's nature and define it by the type of *yetzer* he has chosen. What constitutes "good" and "evil" are *a priori* assumptions made by the Talmud and the Torah based upon their views of the proper and improper ways to fulfill these needs. Such descriptive labels can then be imposed *post hoc* on incidents of behavior which merit the appropriate judgment. The use of the dual-*yetzer* model thereby serves the interests of promoting a heuristic metapsychology and a sound education system. *The problem of human nature is a pragmatic one, not only a scientific or theological one, because it depends on the kind of world we want to live in and bring about.* The choice of whether man is basically good or evil is itself a self-fulfilling prophecy: man can be aggressive when he seeks to maximize his sense of being at the expense of others. Or, if suitable channels are made available, self-maximization can be accomplished in kindness and inter-personal harmony. The Jewish world-view does make such provisions and therefore considers man responsible for the eventual value of his nature.*

---

\* Inasmuch as my examination here involves the halachic concept of sin as some psychiatric construct, I have since detailed further thoughts on the matter, in other directions, in "Mental Illness as Sin; Sin as Neurosis," *Journal of Jewish Communal Service*, 1978, 54 (2).

## NOTES

1. Herford, R., *The Pharisees*, Boston: Beacon, 1952, p. 155–156.
2. Hirsch, W., *Rabbinic Psychology*, London: Goldstone, 1947, p. 216–230.
3. Levi, L., "Towards a Torah-based Psychology," *Proceedings of the Association of Orthodox Jewish Scientists*, II, 1970, p. 98–102. Solomon, A., "Eros-Thanatos: a Modification in the Light of Torah Teachings," *Tradition*, 14(2), 1973, pp. 95–96. The 18th and 19th century Mussar Movement also maintained that the *yetzer hara* was some kind of natural human instinct — see Rachlis, A., "The Mussar Movement and Psychotherapy," *Judaism*, 23(2), 1974, p. 339. One will notice this tendency especially in the writings of Rabbi Yisroel Salanter and Rabbi E. E. Dessler.
4. Bakan, D., *Sigmund Freud and the Jewish Mystical Tradition*, New York: Schocken, 1965. cf. M. Roberts, *From Oedipus to Moses: Freud's Jewish Identity*, New York: Anchor/Doubleday, 1976.
5. This belief stems, of course, from the idea that man was created *Imago Dei*. See I. Epstein, *The Faith of Judaism*, London: Soncino, 1954, p. 200–213. See also Tillich's "What is Basic in Human Nature?" *Humanitas*, 1968, 4(1), p. 91–100, where he discusses his view that what is indeed the basic man is his "finite freedom" i.e., man's ability to choose within the given confines of his own nature and environment. After reading through my contribution, the reader might attempt to understand the polarity of the two *yetzarim* as characterizing the overt manifestations of this continual life struggle between man's finitude versus the aspirations born of his intractable sense of freedom.
6. Krantz, D. L. & Allen, D., "The Rise and Fall of Macdougall's Instinct Doctrine," *The Journal of the History of the Behavioral Sciences*, 3, 1967, pp. 326–338.
7. Skinner, B. F., *About Behaviorism*, New York: Knopf, 1974, p. 11.
8. *Ibid.*, p. 149.
9. *Ibid.*, p. 239.
10. Heschel, A. J., *Who is Man?* California: Stanford University, 1965, p. 7.
11. *Ibid.*, p. 7; 9; 57.
12. Becker, E., *Angel in Armor*, New York: Free Press, 1969, p. 165.
13. Cf. Krantz, *op. cit.*, 1967, *loc. cit.*
14. Becker, *op. cit.*, 1969, p. 165.
15. Schechter, S., *Aspects of Rabbinic Theology*, New York: Schocken, 196 led., pp. 242–243. Sharfman (*Pentateuch: Linear Translation*, New York: SS & R, 1949) translates *y* here as "imagination". Cf. also Fromm's translation in *You Shall Be as Gods*, New York: Fawcett, 1966, p. 126.
16. Schechter, *ibid.*, p. 242.
17. Genesis 8:21. As paraphrased in the Talmud Ber. 61b "Even in his state as a minor, man's thoughts are evil."
18. I Chron. 28:9; and see Schechter, *op. cit.*, pp. 242–243.
19. Genesis 2:7.
20. Talmud Berachot 61a, 54a; T. J. Ber. 3:5.
21. Kiddushin 30b.
22. Canticles Rabbah 7:13.
23. Aboth d'Rav Nathan 16:3; cf. Genesis Rabbah 14:3, however, which states that even

animals have a *yh*. Similarly, in Genesis Rabbah 14:34: ". . . if a man pursues evil, he is likened to an animal."

24. P'sikta Rabbati 9:2.
25. Zohar Tosefta ii, 69b.
26. Genesis 1:31.
27. Genesis Rabbah 9:9; Eccl. Rabbah 3:15.
28. *Encyclopedia Judaica*, New York: Macmillan, 1971, VIII: 1318.
29. Solomon, *op. cit.*, 1973, pp. 95–96.
30. As R. Chananiah b. Dosa said, "It is not the ferocious ass which kills, it is sin which kills" (Berachot 33a); cf. also Genesis Rabbah 8:11: ". . . if man sin, he will die, and if not: he shall live," and Ezekiel 18:4.
31. Solomon, *op. cit.*, p. 97.
32. See Talmud Yoma 69b. I am equating the Talmud's statement, that without the *yh* man would never engage in business, with some sort of concept of an aggression impulse.
33. Freud, S., *An Outline of Psychoanalysis*, New York: Norton, 1949, p. 5.
34. Solomon, *op. cit.*, p. 95.
35. *Ibid.*, p. 96.
36. Blum, G., *Psychoanalytic Theories of Personality*, New York: McGraw-Hill, 1953. Freud also believed that the aggressive impulse was beyond the pleasure principle (*der lustprincipes*) in the sense that the discharge of aggression, unlike that of libido, is unaccompanied by pleasure in and of itself. However, the neo-Freudian view, expressed by Hartmann, *et al.*, is that aggression bears the same relation to pleasure and unpleasure as does libido; viz., discharge of aggression gives rise to pleasure while accumulation and lack of discharge of aggression gives rise to unpleasure. See Hartmann, H., Kris, E. & Lowenstein, R., "Notes on the Theory of Aggression," *Psychoanalytic Study of the Child*, 1949, 3–43, and Brenner, C., "The Psychoanalytic Concept of Aggression," *International J. Psychoanalysis*, 1971, 52, p. 140.
37. Nuttin, J., *Psychoanalysis and Personality*, New York: Mentor, 1962, p. 82–83.
38. Holzman, P., *Psychoanalysis and Psychopathology*, New York: McGraw-Hill, 1970, p. 113. Waelder, R., *Basic Theory of Psychoanalysis*, New York: Schocken, 1960, p. 98–103. Also noted in Chessick, R., *Intensive Psychotherapy*, New York: Aronson, 1974, p. 37.
39. *Ibid.*, p. 114. Freud himself talked of the "far-reaching instinctive endowment of animals . . . if (only) human beings too possessed an instinctive knowledge such as this" (Freud, S., *The Unconscious*, Standard Words, Hogarth, 1915, 14, p. 195).
40. Waelder, *op. cit.*, p. 146.
41. Holzman, *op. cit.*, p. 128–129. See S. Freud, Beyond the Pleasure Principle, *Standard Edition of the Complete Works of S. Freud*, p. 3–66, Vol. XVIII, London: Hogarth.
42. *Ibid.*, p. 113.
43. Schechter, *op. cit.*, p. 244 quotes Eccl. Rabbah 4:14, ". . . the foolish old king to whom all the organs (sic) of the body show obedience." This might have been an interesting ground for evidence of the endosomatic root of the *yh*. Unfortunately, however — and surprisingly, at least as far as my re-checking of the various MSs of that midrashic corpus reveal — Schechter has misquoted, as the quotation in the *loc. cit* states

"*she'hakol shomim lo*", "all *mankind* hearken to it (the *yh*)". However, cf. Kallah Rabbati 3, "Every sin of man is engraved in his bones."

44. Sanhedrin 91b.

45. Eccl. Rabbah 4:15. Other sources say not until the age of ten, or thirteen, does a child sin.

46. Cf. note 24.

47. Holzman, *op. cit.*, p. 133.

48. "Who is mighty? He who subdues his *yetzer*," *Ethics of the Fathers* 4:1.

49. Canticles Rabbah 7:13; Genesis Rabbah 9:9; Eccl. Rabbah 3:15.

50. Waelder, *op. cit.*, p. 105.

51. Blum, *op. cit.*, p. 16.

52. Nuttin, *op. cit.*, p. 71.

53. *Ibid.*, pp. 79–80.

54. *Ibid.*, p. 192.

55. See my discussion in "Anxiety and Religious Growth: A Talmudic Perspective," *Journal of Religion and Health*, 1977, 16(1), p. 52-58.

56. Hirsch, S. R. *The Pentateuch*, Isaac Levy (trans.), England, L. Honig & Sons, 1959 ed., p. 165.

57. *Ibid.*, ch. 6:5. See also the commentary of O. Seforno on Exodus 20:5 ("I visit the sins of the fathers upon the sons, and so on the third and on the fourth generations") where he states: "He will visit the sins . . . only when the sons persist in their fathers' actions, and they thus *add to the ideal of their hearts* (*u'mosifim yetzer machshevot libam*)." That is to say, if I am correct, again, that one consciously designs to make evil one's ideal. This sort of excursis is quite compatible with Hirsch's and points to the non-instinctivist approach to understanding the *yh*.

58. Such as Fromm, Maslow, Erikson, May, Sartre and Binswanger.

59. Fromm, E., *The Anatomy of Human Destructiveness*, New York: Fawcett, 1973, II and *passim*.

60. Becker, *op. cit.*, 1969, p. 173.

61. Becker, E., *The Denial of Death*, New York: Free Press, 1973, p. 53, 57.

62. Eruvin 13b.

63. Heschel, *op. cit.*, p. 10.

64. Eccl. Rabbah 3:15.

65. Zohar Tosefta ii:64b.

# THE FREE ENTERPRISE MODEL:
# A HALAKHIC PERSPECTIVE

AARON LEVINE

Production, exchange, and consumption lie at the heart of society's economic activities. Devising a mechanism to organize, regulate and integrate these activities constitutes the basic economic problem confronting every society. Tradition, authoritative direction and the free enterprise system are representative of societal approaches to the problem of economic organization.

Under the free enterprise approach, the spontaneous, free interplay of market forces determines the mix of products the economic system produces; its methods of production and exchange; and its patterns of income distribution.

The efficiency of the system is predicated on the attainment of certain conditions in each and every microeconomic market. These conditions include the following: (1) a semblance of perfect knowledge on the part of all economic actors; (2) many buyers and sellers in each industry; (3) homogeneous outputs in each industry; (4) homogeneity in input markets; (5) freedom of entry in each industry; (6) perfect mobility of resources.

Social welfare is maximized when the economy's income is maximized and its consumers command the largest possible volume and variety of products and services with their given money income. Advocates of the free enterprise economy assert that when the above conditions obtain, this ideal is realized.

Why the free enterprise system promotes social welfare is explained by

*Rabbi Dr. Aaron Levine was ordained and studied at the* Kolel *of the Rabbi Jacob Joseph Rabbinical Seminary in New York. He received his Ph.D. in economics from New York University and is presently Chairman of the Department of Economics at Yeshiva University.*

*Under a research grant from the Memorial Foundation for Jewish Culture, Dr. Levine is studying economics as described in Jewish sources. He is also Editor of* Kol Yaakov, *a Hebrew periodical concerning Jewish law published by the Rabbi Jacob Joseph Rabbinical Seminary. An earlier essay by Dr. Levine entitled "Equity in Taxation as Discussed in Rabbinic Literature" appeared in the April 1976 issue of* Intercom.

the workings of the competitive process. Within the idealized framework of the free enterprise economy, abnormal profits in any particular industry would be a transient phenomenon. Alert resource owners would withdraw from their present endeavors and switch to the advantaged industry. With supply increasing relative to demand in the advantaged area, prices and profit margins would be expected to fall there. Simultaneously, the decrease in supply, *ceteris parabus*, in the disadvantaged sectors would tend to increase prices and profit margins there. These adjustments thus tend to narrow the original differential.

Changes in relative prices act as a powerful stimulus for resource owners to expand output in those areas where supply is scarce relative to demand and contract output where the situation is in reverse. The workings of the competitive process thus give rise to the paradox that the pursuit of self-interest results in the maximization of social welfare.[1]

This article will investigate the degree of freedom a Torah-directed society enjoys in adopting the free enterprise approach as an *operational blueprint* for its mode of economic organization. While it is clear that halakha expresses no inherent preference for a particular form of economic organization,[2] both the marketplace and market conduct in the Torah-directed society, as discussed below, are subject to regulation and ethical prescriptions. Particular aspects of the free enterprise model that will be given attention in this article include:   (1) the extent to which the Torah allows the free interplay of market forces to determine price and profit margins in the various markets;   (2) the validity of the operational assumption of perfect knowledge in light of halakhic regulations of economic relationships; and   (3) the extent to which halakha promotes freedom of entry.

CONTROL OF PRICES AND WAGES

A Jewish community, as a collective, is regarded halakhically as having the legislative status of a *beth din* or king.[3] Communal enactments, properly legislated, are therefore binding on all members of the community, including minors and even those not yet born.[4]

One communal legislative prerogative explicitly mentioned in the Talmud is price and wage regulation.[5] Such legislation becomes effective law, according to *Mabit*, by means of a simple majority of those eligible to vote.[6]

The scope of the community's authority in price and wage matters is quite extensive. All input and output markets are potentially subject to such regulation. Vendors may be required to sell their products within a specified time period. In addition, communal legislation may direct vendors not to sell their wares outside the town's limits.[7]

Notwithstanding its broad authoritative scope in controlling prices and wages, the community may very well opt to leave certain of its markets unregulated.[8] Failure to set prices in particular markets effectively allows the free interplay of supply and demand to determine price in those segments of its economy.

The option of leaving prices unregulated is, however, not open to the community in relation to commodities essential to human life (*chayei nefesh*). By Rabbinical decree, a profit rate limitation of one-sixth[9] is set for vendors dealing in such commodities.[10]

Which commodities are to be regarded as essential and hence subject to regulation is a matter of dispute. The controversy centers around the interpretation *offered by Rambam* (*Yad, Hilkhot Mechirah*, XIV:2) of the following definition of a regulated commodity:

> The vendor is proscribed from earning more than one-sixth profit. When does this apply? only to commodities essential to life, i.e., wine, oil, and flour. However, in regard to roots, i.e., costus and frankincense, and the like, no price is fixed and the vendor may earn as much profit as he desires.

*Maggid Mishnah* interprets the first part of the above definition strictly, while the latter part is taken by him loosely. Only foodstuff itself is to be regarded as essential to life and, hence, subject to regulation. What follows from this understanding of the text is that products essential for the *preparation* of food (*makhshirei okhel nefesh*) are not subject to price regulation.[11]

A diametrically opposite interpretation of the above text is advanced by *Bet Yosef*. Only products not essential even in the preparation of foodstuff, i.e., roots, are not subject to regulation. Commodities used in the preparation of foodstuff are considered as foodstuff itself and subject to price control.[12]

A third taxonomy is offered by *Semah*. While vendors of foodstuff are subject to a one-sixth profit rate limitation, the allowable profit margin is widened up to 100% for sellers of products used in preparation of foodstuff. Finally, products not even used in the preparation of foodstuff need not be regulated at all.[13]

The cost elements that enter into the base against which the allowable profit rate is applied include all the explicit expenses the vendor incurs in the process of selling his product. Besides his cost price, these outlays might consist of storage and portage costs as well.[14] Should the sale of the product require the vendor to provide his labor services on a continuous basis, i.e., a retailer, the cost base, according to *Meiri, Rosh*, and *Tur*, expands to include an allowance for his toil and trouble as well.[15] No return for implicit wages appears in the cost base, however, when the sale of the product does not require the vendor to provide his labor services on a continuous basis, i.e., a wholesaler.[16]

Including a return for labor services in the cost base effectively allows the vendor to earn the allowable one-sixth profit rate on his invested capital and on his labor services as well.

The above conceptualization of the cost base is not universally held. Other *Rishonim* view the one-sixth profit rate as a return the vendor earns for the labor services he provides in the process of selling his product. No allowance for a return on invested capital is called for according to this view. What follows is that when continuous labor services are not rendered in the process of selling the product, the product must be sold at its cost price, that is at a zero profit margin.[17]

Formulating the allowable profit rate in the above manner does not, however, eliminate entirely the possibility of earning profits for the middleman. This follows from the fact that the one-sixth profit rate constraint does not apply when the current market price rises above the level that prevailed at the time the middleman purchased his merchandise. For example, suppose a middleman bought wheat at harvest time at $2 a bushel. Now, a month later, the market price of wheat rises to $4 a bushel. Given the rise in the market price, the middleman may sell his wheat at $4 a bushel, notwithstanding the 66 2/3% mark up he realizes thereby.[18]

Moreover, the one-sixth profit constraint is binding on the individual seller only when the industry in general adheres to this rule. Should the rule be generally ignored, however, even the seller willing to submit to the authority of halakha is not ethically bound to it.[19] Given the insignificant portion of the total market demand the submissive seller serves, directing him to conform with the profit rate rule would generate little impact on consumer welfare. The economic interests of the submissive seller are therefore given primacy by allowing him to follow the general trade practice.[20]

CONTROL OF MARKET CONDUCT

Price and wage legislation represents a direct means of controlling market price. This same objective could be achieved by means of regulating market conduct. Given that market price is determined by the interaction of aggregate demand and supply forces, mandated patterns of *market conduct* exert a definite impact on the nature of the relationship between these aggregates and hence influence the direction of market price.

Market conduct is a subject of halakhic prescription. Regulations designed to discourage the proliferation of middlemen and restrictions against hoarding are examples of halakhic prescriptions intended to increase supply relative to demand.

Halakhic restrictions against hoarding take the form of disallowing market purchases of essential commodities in excess of normal consumption needs. Producers, though, may normally withhold any part of their crop from market sale. Nonetheless, during a period of famine, producers are subject to a quota in regard to the amount of produce they may store. The quota allows the producer to store no more than one year's supply of foodstuff for himself and his family.[21]

To insure a plentiful supply of essential products in the land of Israel, the Sages required producers to sell their products directly to consumers.[22] Middlemen are not entitled to a mark-up unless they work to process the product they purchased. Processing wheat into flour is an example of an activity that entitles a middleman to a mark-up.[23]

With the same objective in mind, the Sages prohibited the exporting or transferring of essential produce from Israel.[24] Included in the interdict is the prohibition against exporting from one province to another within the geographic boundaries of Israel.[25]

Reducing demand relative to supply represents still another means of effecting a reduction in market price. The classical example of how the Sages effected a reduction in market price by artificially manipulating the aggregated demand schedule is recorded in the Mishnah Keritut 1:7. Noting the exhorbitant price of birds of the type needed for the fulfillment of the sacrificial requirements of women who gave birth, R. Simeon b. Gamliel the Elder set out to remedy the situation. Motivated by a grave concern that the exorbitant price of these birds could lead to a wholesale neglect of the sacrificial obligation, this Sage boldly *changed*[26] the law governing the sacrificial requirements of women who gave birth. To this end he proclaimed that a woman who had five definite births need bring one sacrifice only and would thereby become ritually pure. Formerly, each birth required a separate sacrifice. The effect of the proclamation was quite dramatic. With the demand for sacrificial birds dropping off markedly, their price gravitated to a reasonable level.

An even more drastic means of effecting a reduction in market price via manipulation of aggregate demand is the consumer boycott. *Zemach Zedek* gave explicit sanction to the use of this tactic by the town of Nikolsburg, Moravia against its local fishmongers. These vendors, "having seen that the Jews were not deterred by expensive prices from buying fish for the Sabbath," decided to charge an exorbitant price for their product. Rejecting the notion that the boycott in some measure slighted the honor of the Sabbath, *Zemach Zedek* ruled that in order to enable also the poor "to honor the Sabbath by (eating) fish" it would be better not to buy fish for a few Sabbaths so as to bring down the prices. Finally, the legitimacy of the boycott tactic is defended on the basis of the Mishnah in Keritut 1:7, cited above.[27]

Another important insight into the workings of the market mechanism found in Talmudic literature is the notion that what determines market price is not the actual conditions of relative scarcity, but rather how these conditions are *subjectively* perceived by market participants. Given the subjective element in price determination, producers could very well decide to raise price in response to false signals they receive regarding actual conditions of relative scarcity.

Realization of the above phenomenon led the Sages, according to *Rashi*, *Tur*, and *Magen Avraham*, to rule that proclamation of a public fast on account of draught should not be announced for the first time on a Thursday. Initiating the public fast on Thursday would significantly increase the normal level of demand for this day. Households would stock up for both their meal at the termination of the fast and for their Sabbath requirements. Vendors, not understanding the basis of the sudden surge in demand, would interpret it as a frantic scramble to buy up the available food supply in anticipation of a drastic future cut in this supply. Given this evaluation of the situation, sellers would spontaneously raise their prices. To avoid this unnecessary increase in price, the public fast is initiated for the first time on a Tuesday. Here, the resultant change in the normal pattern of demand would not be very large as Sabbath orders are not, in any case, placed on this day. With no false signals sent, prices would not rise.[28]

The welfare of the business sector was also a vital concern of the Sages. Appreciation of the fact that the viability of the community's economic life hinges heavily upon the prosperity of the business sector finds expression in the following Talmudic passage in Baba Batra 91a:

Our Rabbis taught: Public prayers are offered for goods (which have become dangerously cheap), even on the Sabbath. R. Yochanan said: For instance: linen garments in Babylon and wine and oil in Palestine. R. Joseph said: This (is only so) when (these have become so) cheap that ten are sold at (the price of) six.

THE FREE ENTERPRISE MODEL AND PERFECT KNOWLEDGE

Much of the optimizing nature of the free enterprise economy, as discussed in the introduction, is predicated on the presumption of complete rationality and perfect knowledge on the part of all market participants.

To the extent that the realities of economic life belie the validity of the idealized model of the free enterprise system, the market mechanism is neither self-regulating nor an adequate protective agency against human avarice.

Indeed, the complex nature of modern commerce has forced free enterprise advocates to temper somewhat their faith in the validity of the presumption of perfect knowledge on the part of market participants. Today, buyer and seller no longer contract on a footing of equality. Consumers are deemed ill-equipped to judge quality and correctness of measure. Driven more and more to rely on the honesty, skill and judgment of the seller, the buyer, it is conceded, must be protected against fraud. Nonetheless, the presumption that the consumer is both aware of the existence of price differentials and the alternative market opportunities open to him remain, according to free enterprise advocates, valid today.

The Torah does not regard the idealized version of the free enterprise model as descriptive of the realities of economic life. That the presumption of perfect knowledge is held invalid by the Torah is clearly evidenced by the comprehensive scope of halakhic regulation of the buyer-seller relationship. The self-regulating mechanism of the market system is not relied upon to insure the honesty of the vendor in the design and use of his weights and measures. Rather, halakha sets standards here and provides for a system of inspection.[29]

Similarly, what facts buyer and seller disclose to each other pertinent to their transaction is not left to their individual discretions, but rather is halakhically specified.[30] Finally, halakha provides a taxonomy of grounds for invalidating or otherwise modifying market transactions on account of price[31] and quality[32] fraud.

Insofar as free enterprise proponents recognize the need for consumer protection against quality fraud of various kinds, halakhic prescription in this area is quite consistent with the spirit of this school of thought. Nevertheless, halakhic negation of the presumption of the awareness of the existence of price differentials is not consistent with the free enterprise approach.

THE VALIDITY OF THE ASSUMPTION OF PERFECT KNOWLEDGE IN LIGHT OF HALAKHIC REGULATIONS

Individuals freely entering into a market transaction are presumed, halakhically, to have an approximate notion of the value of the article involved. Hence, price agreements which diverge enormously from the prevailing norm are not regarded as having occurred as a result of ignorance of market conditions on the part of the participants involved. Divergent price agreements are, quite to the contrary, interpreted as representing a tacit understanding between buyer and seller to treat the price differential as a voluntary gift transfer.[33]

When the discrepancy between the sale price and the prevailing norm falls within the margin of error, the laws pertaining to *ona'ah* or price fraud become applicable. Though constituting a separate interdict, an *ona'ah* offense is regarded by the Torah as a violation of property rights and is classified as a form of *gezel* (robbery).[34] Three degrees of *ona'ah* have been identified by the Sages:

(I) First degree *ona'ah* occurs when the discrepancy between the sale price and the market price is more than one-sixth. Here, grounds exist for invalidating the original sale.[35] Nullification rights in the above case, according to *Rambam* and *Bet Yosef*, rest exclusively with the plaintiff. Should the latter express a desire to uphold the transaction, despite the *ona'ah*, the offender must accept this and may not, in turn, invalidate the sale.[36] Selecting this option does not, however, avail the plaintiff to any claim for the restoration of the *ona'ah* involved. Plaintiff may either void the transaction or accept it as it was originally concluded.[37]

Another opinion in the above matter is expressed by *Rabbeinu Yonah*. In his view, as long as the plaintiff does not uphold the transaction, the offender too is given the prerogative of voiding it. The offender's rights in this matter proceed from the magnitude of the *ona'ah* involved. Since the concluded price diverged more than one-sixth from the market price, the offender may claim that the original transaction should be treated as an agreement consummated in error (*mekach Ta-ut*). Once the transaction is upheld by the plaintiff, the offender loses his right to void the sale. Denying the offender full nullification rights here follows from the fact that he, the offender, enjoys no such right when his offense consists of the less severe crime of contracting for a sale price involving less than first degree *ona'ah*. Conferring him with full nullification rights when his offense is graver runs counter to all canons of equity (*shelo yehei choteh niskar*).[38]

(II)  Second degree *ona'ah* occurs when the sale price differs from the market price by exactly one-sixth. Here, the transaction remains binding. Neither of the parties involved may subsequently void the transaction on account of the *ona'ah*. The plaintiff, however, is entitled to full restitution of the *ona'ah* involved.[39]

(III)  Finally, third degree *ona'ah* occurs when the sale price differs from the market price by less than one-sixth. Here, the transaction not only remains binding but, in addition, the plaintiff has no legal claim to the price differential.[40]

The absence of any provision for legal redress in case (III) leads *Rosh* to speculate whether it might be permissible, in the first instance, to contract into third degree *ona'ah*. Pivotal to the resolution of this question, in *Rosh*'s view, is the definition of market price. Is market price to be understood as a single value, or is it to be defined as the *range of deviations of less than one-sixth from the prevailing norm*? Adopting the former view leads to the conclusion that knowledge of the market norm prohibits either party from contracting into a price agreement that diverges even slightly from it. The absence of legal redress for third degree *ona'ah* would then be explained by the presumption that when the degree of *ona'ah* involved is of such a relatively small amount, the plaintiff waives his legal claim to restitution. This presumption follows from our inability to precisely fix the value of the article sold. While some experts would insist that *ona'ah* took place, others would just as vehemently deny it. With experts divided as to whether *ona'ah* occurred, and if it did by how much, we may safely presume that the victim of this possible *ona'ah* waives his legal right to restitution.

Adopting the latter view, however, leads to the conclusion that third degree *ona'ah* is not price fraud at all. Denying legal restitution here follows from the fact that the concluded price, though at variance with the prevailing norm, falls, nevertheless, within the *legal* price range. Why price should be defined as a range of values rather than by the prevailing norm is defended by *Rosh* on the grounds that even when both buyer and seller are fully aware of the prevailing norm, each would on occasion contract, to their own disadvantage, into a price agreement at variance with this norm. The vendor, for instance, would offer to sell his wares below the prevailing market price when the merchandise at hand represents unwanted inventory, or when he has an urgent need to raise cash. Similarly, the buyer, finding a product to his keen liking would, on occasion, offer to pay for it a price above the market norm. Given these facts, market price should not be properly defined as a single value, but rather as a range of deviations around this value.

Though offering no definitive halakhic resolution of the above dilemma, *Rosh* urges the following guideline for cases of third degree *ona'ah*: Cognizant of the prevailing norm, an individual should not contract into a price agreement that even departs slightly from this value. Should an individual fall victim to third degree *ona'ah*, on the other hand, he should accept his loss graciously and express no complaint.[41]

The uncertainty of *Rosh* regarding why third degree *ona'ah* is *legally* not subject to return is not shared by other *Rishonim* (early codifiers of Jewish law). *Rambam*, *Tur* and *Mechaber* understand the lack of restitution provisions here as stemming from a presumption that the plaintiff waives[42] his claims against the offender when the degree of *ona'ah* involved is relatively small, i.e., third degree.[43] What follows as a corollary, according to *Rosh*'s line of reasoning, is a prohibition against *knowingly* contracting into third degree *ona'ah*. This latter action is explicitly prohibited by Rambam.[44]

Finding a need to provide the producer with a strong economic incentive to insure a plentiful supply of staple commodities in every locality, *Sefer Hachinuch* explicitly permits an individual to knowingly contract into third degree *ona'ah*.[45]

Implicit in *Rosh*'s analysis of third degree *ona'ah*, according to *Arukh Hashulchan*, is the proposition that plaintiff's restitution claims are denied in this case only when the product market involved is *heterogeneous in nature*. *Rosh*'s explanation of why it is reasonable to assume that plaintiff waives his claims against the offender in third degree *ona'ah* cases convincingly forces this conclusion. The basis of this presumption, as will be recalled, is the division among experts as to whether or not *ona'ah* took place. Now, this disagreement among experts is only comprehensible when the product market involved is heterogeneous in nature. Determining whether or not *ona'ah* took place by means of consulting experts is obviously unnecessary when the product market involved is standardized and homogeneous. Here, price uniformity would make the occurrence of *ona'ah* immediately apparent. With the occurrence of *ona'ah* not subject to dispute when the product market is homogeneous, the presumption that the plaintiff waives his claims of restitution is not defensible regardless of the inconsequential nature of the *ona'ah* involved.[46]

Halakha places all victims of *ona'ah* on an equal footing. No distinction is made between the casual market participant and the shrewd dealer. When victims of *ona'ah* are entitled to restitution or nullification rights, these rights apply even when the plaintiff turns out to be a shrewd businessman. Business acumen does not generate a halakhic presumption of awareness of the market norm at the moment the sale was consummated. Conversely, no special considerations or additional rights are conferred on the novice or infrequent market participant when he is victimized by *ona'ah*.[47]

Insofar as legal remedies against *ona'ah* are rationalized on the presumption of ignorance of market conditions, the plaintiff's restitution and nullification rights do not extend over an indefinite period of time.

When the buyer is defrauded, a lapse of sufficient time to allow him the opportunity to show his purchase to an expert assessor forfeits for him any legal recourse against *ona'ah*.[48] This time span provides the plaintiff with sufficient time to ascertain whether or not his purchase involved *ona'ah*. Silence beyond this interval is therefore taken as an implicit waiver of his legal claim against *ona'ah*.[49]

When an article is purchased on credit, silence beyond the legal limit on the part of the buyer is not, however, construed as an implicit waiver of his legal rights against *ona'ah*. Here the buyer may defend his prolonged silence on the grounds that since he did not yet make payment he was not particular to investigate whether the purchase involved *ona'ah*. Nonetheless, once the credit buyer uses his article of purchase, his extended rights against *ona'ah* expire.[50]

When the seller is defrauded, he may exercise his legal claim against the buyer until time elapses sufficient for him to ascertain the market price of the goods he sold. Should the article involved not be generally available in the marketplace, the seller's *ona'ah* claims extend until we are certain he witnessed a market sale of an article of the same type involved in the *ona'ah* transaction.[51]

Though the plaintiff's right against *ona'ah* proceeds from the presumption that he was ignorant of the prevailing norm at the time he entered into the transaction, certainty that he was aware of this norm at that time does not automatically invalidate his subsequent claims against the offender. The offender escapes with impunity only when it can be presumed that the plaintiff waived all claims against him in the matter. Hence, a victim of second degree *ona'ah* retains restitution rights against the offender even when it can be established that he was aware of the market norm at the time the sale was finalized. Here, far from constituting an implicit waiver of his rights, the plaintiff's failure to register any complaint when he negotiated the sale could very well manifest on his part an artful design against the offender. Viewing his options, the plaintiff could indeed have concluded that his optimal stratagem required him to *delay* his protest until after the sale was finalized. Demanding that the transaction be concluded at the market norm might provoke the offender to break off negotiations altogether. Bargaining with him, on the other hand, to reduce the price differential might prove successful, but would at the same time reduce the degree of *ona'ah* involved from second to third degree. With no restitution rights provided for the plaintiff in third degree *ona'ah* cases, pursuit of this course of action would effectively disallow him to recover the differential. Most attractive to him would therefore be to allow the sale to be concluded with second degree *ona'ah*. Once it was finalized, he would then assert his restitution rights.

A variation of the above case occurs when the concluded sale involves first degree *ona'ah*. In this instance, certainty that the plaintiff was aware of the prevailing norm at the time he entered into the sale invalidates his subsequent claims against the offender. Insofar as first degree *ona'ah* cases do not generate restitution rights for the plaintiff, his silence at the time he entered into the sale cannot be construed as a ploy to recover the price differential involved. The plaintiff's failure to protest is therefore taken as an implicit waiver of his claims against *ona'ah*.[52]

### THE BASIS OF THE ONA'AH CLAIM

The basis of the *ona'ah* claim requires further exploration. Given both the assumption of rationality and the voluntary nature of the agreement, would the plaintiff have freely entered into the original transaction unless he felt certain he was receiving in exchange equivalent *subjective value*? What then is the basis of his subsequent *ona'ah* claim? Strategic to the resolution of the above dilemma is the halakhic presumption of what the buyer and seller intend to accomplish with their transaction. Under the supposition that the basic intent of parties to a transaction is to exchange values of *equal objective* or market worth, the legitimacy of the *ona'ah* claim is readily apparent. Given the above presumption of intent, any discrepancy between the transaction price and the market norm signifies that the original objective was not realized. That the plaintiff's subjective evaluation of the object he purchased bears no relevancy in assessing his subsequent *ona'ah* claim is clearly evidenced by the following Talmudic passage in Baba Metzia 58b:

> It has been taught: R. Judah said, the sale of a scroll of law, too, is not subject to *ona'ah* because its value is unlimited; an animal or pearl is not subject to *ona'ah* because one desires to match them. Said they (the Sages) to him, but one wishes to match up everything. And R. Judah? – these are particularly important to him (the purchaser); others are not. And to what extent? Said Amemar: Up to their value.

Why the Sages reject the relevancy of the plaintiff's subjective evaluation of the article he purchased in assessing the *ona'ah* claim is understandable under the thesis that what legitimizes the *ona'ah* claim is the presumption that the original transaction intended to exchange values of equal objective or market value. What follows as a corollary from the above argument is that even an explicit declaration on the part of the plaintiff that the article he is acquiring is subjectively worth to him the entire sum demanded by the seller does not invalidate his subsequent *ona'ah* claims.

The Sages' reply to R. Judah, "but one wishes to match up everything," is of particular interest to the history of economic thought. Implicit in this rebuttal is an anticipation of the economic concept of consumer surplus. This notion is concerned with the relationship between market price and subjective value. Market price is, today, understood to be the result of the interplay of *aggregate* supply and demand forces. Price is determined *outside* the influence of the individual producer or consumer. The price an individual consumer would be willing to pay to obtain a given product may not coincide with this market price. When the consumer's subjective evaluation of the product falls below this price, he obviously rejects the product. When his subjective evaluation of the product either coincides with or exceeds the market price, the consumer will buy the product. In the latter instance, he will enjoy a windfall as well. The difference between the maximum price the consumer would willingly pay to obtain the product, rather than do without it, and the actual transaction price provides a measure of this windfall or consumer surplus. Does a given market price generate at least some amount of consumer surplus to the great majority of those patronizing the product at that price? Economic theory answers in the affirmative. The prevailing norm represents the market's evaluation of the last unit of the commodity in question offered for sale. Assuming diminishing marginal utility, this evaluation will afford consumer surplus to the great majority of the actual patrons of the product.

With the market price of the commodity affording some consumer surplus to a vast number of its patrons, the underlying logic of the Sages rejecting R. Judah's view becomes apparent. Just as *ona'ah* claims are normally not negated on account of the presumed consumer surplus above market price enjoyed by the plaintiff, so too the *ona'ah* claim should not be discarded when the article of purchase was an animal or pearl. Granted that the consumer surplus generated in the latter cases could be considerable, as the buyer could well have intended to match his purchase with a similar item he already had, nonetheless, the *possible magnitude* of the consumer surplus involved is *entirely irrelevant* as far as the *ona'ah* claim is concerned. This irrelevancy follows from the fact that the legitimacy of the *ona'ah* claim is not based on any presumed discrepancy between subjective value and the transaction price, but rather on the supposition that the original transaction intended to exchange values of equal objective worth. Given that the above objective was not realized, the validity of the *ona'ah* claim remains unquestioned.

### THE BASIS OF THE ONA'AH CLAIM — ANOTHER VIEW

The basis of the *ona'ah* claim is apparently understood by *Ritva* in a different light. This follows from his unusual ruling that should the buyer declare at the time of the sale that his purchase is subjectively worth to him the entire sum demanded by the seller, he thereby forfeits any subsequent *ona'ah* claim against the seller.[53] Now, supposing that the intent of parties to a transaction is to exchange values of equal *objective* worth, why should such a declaration forfeit for the buyer his *ona'ah* claim against the seller?

*Ritva*'s ruling, in our view, can be understood in the following light: The legitimacy of the *ona'ah* claim is based on a presumed variance between the original transaction price and the *true* subjective value the plaintiff attaches to the article exchanged.

Obviously, *true* subjective value can only be determined under conditions of perfect knowledge. Given the presumption that the plaintiff was unaware of the prevailing norm at the time he entered into the original agreement, the *ona'ah* price he willingly agreed to pay or offer for the product cannot be said to measure the true subjective value he attaches to it.

For the seller, whose motive in the transaction is to convert his product into cash, the market price serves admirably as a measure of the purchasing power, or subjective value he could obtain for it. The *ona'ah* claim of the seller is hence based on the assertion that the original transaction did not provide him with subjective equivalence. What follows naturally from this interpretation of *Ritva*'s position is *Rosh*'s explanation of why third degree *ona'ah* claims by the seller are denied. Given that the seller, finding himself pressed for cash, would willingly sell his product below market price, his claim that he did not receive equivalent subjective value in the original transaction is denied when the amount of *ona'ah* involved is merely third degree.

For the buyer, the maximum price he would pay for the product rather than do without it provides a monetary measure of the subjective value he attaches to his purchase. Given the presumption that he was unaware of the market price at the time he entered into the original transaction, the *ona'ah* price he willingly paid to obtain his purchase cannot be said to accurately measure his true subjective valuation of the product. Without knowing how the market values the product, he is incapable of gauging with any degree of accuracy his own subjective attitudes and feelings toward the product. Given the discrepancy between the transaction price and the market norm, the plaintiff may subsequently claim that the original transaction failed to provide him with subjective equivalency. Why third degree *ona'ah* claims made by the buyer are denied now becomes abundantly clear. Given the probability that market price affords the plaintiff with some amount of consumer surplus, the latter's protest that the third degree *ona'ah* transaction price he paid failed to provide him with subjective equivalency is rejected outright.

CIRCUMSTANCES UNDER WHICH ONA'AH DOES NOT APPLY

Not all market transactions are subject to the laws of *ona'ah*. Circumstances under which the laws of *ona'ah* are either suspended or modified include the following:

(a) Transactions calling for either the seller or the buyer to waive his claims against *ona'ah* are halakhically valid, despite their effect of contracting out of the laws of *ona'ah*.[54] Escape clauses against *ona'ah* claims derive their validity from the general ruling that contracting out of the laws of the Torah in monetary matters binds the parties to the terms of their agreement.[55] Waiving his rights in the matter does not forfeit for the injured party his claims against *ona'ah* unless his waiver was offered in full knowledge of the price variance involved in the transaction. When the waiver was, however, offered as a *hypothetical gesture*, the injured party retains his claims against *ona'ah*. This follows from the presumption that a hypothetical waiver is tendered out of a sense of security that no *ona'ah* was involved in the transaction. Had the plaintiff been aware of the price differential, he would not have made the gesture at all. Hence, his subsequent claims against *ona'ah* remain intact.[56]

(b)   When a vendor sells his wares on trust (*nosei be'emunah*) he is not subsequently liable to *ona'ah* claims.[57] Selling on trust, according to *Rambam*, requires the vendor to divulge to his prospective buyer his cost price and his proposed profit margin. Should the buyer agree to these terms and consummate the transaction with a *kinyan*, a subsequent finding that the cost price involved *ona'ah* does not allow the plaintiff to modify the original transaction in any manner. Agreeing to allow the vendor a specified profit margin demonstrates on the part of the buyer an unconcern with what the objective market value of the commodity is. Given that realization of the agreed-upon profit rate required the sale to be concluded at the stipulated price, subsequent claims against *ona'ah* are denied.[58]

Selling on trust disallows subsequent *ona'ah* claims only when it is discovered later that the cost price involved *ona'ah*. Should the vendor be aware that his cost involves *ona'ah*, he is obligated to disclose this information to the prospective buyer. Failure to do so is regarded as deceptive conduct on his part. Hence, in the event it can be established that the vendor was aware that his cost price involved *ona'ah*, selling on trust subsequently does not exempt him from *ona'ah* regulations.[59]

(c)   Barter transactions (*chalifin*) are not subject to *ona'ah* regulations. This exemption proceeds from an examination of the textual source of the prohibition against *ona'ah*, *And if thou sell aught unto thy neighbor, or acquirest aught of thy neighbor, ye should not wrong one another.*[60] By use of the term *sell*, the verse is taken to refer solely to money transactions. Barter transactions are hence excluded from *ona'ah* regulations.[61]

*Arukh Hashulchan* rationalizes the above exclusion by pointing out that money transactions differ in essence from barter transactions. When money is the medium of exchange, the clear intent of the parties to the transaction is to exchange equal objective values. Given this intent, the prevailing norm serves admirably to determine whether or not this objective was realized. Barter transactions, on the other hand, are predicated on the existence of a double coincidence of wants. With neither of the articles involved in the exchange constituting a commonly-accepted medium of exchange, the intent of each party is clearly to acquire something of greater subjective value to himself than what he has to offer in exchange. The laws of *ona'ah* therefore do not apply to barter exchanges.

Should an appraisal of the articles involved in the barter be made before or immediately after the exchange is effected, the transaction is subject to *ona'ah* regulation. With the exchange involving appraisal, each party signals an intent to exchange his own object for another of equal *objective* value.

Barter transactions involving produce (*peirot*) are always subject to *ona'ah* regulation. Setting apart produce exchanges from other barter transactions follows from a consideration of the halakhic definition of a barter transaction. For an exchange to be halakhically classified as a barter transaction it must allow A to automatically acquire B's object as soon as B acquires possession of A's object by means of executing the symbolic act (*kinyan*) of drawing A's object to himself (*meshikhah*). When A fails to acquire B's object in this automatic fashion, but instead is required to perform a *kinyan meshikhah* too, the exchange is classified as a sales transaction and not as a barter agreement. A barter exchange involving produce becomes effective by means of this automatic mechanism only when it is accompanied by an appraisal. In the absence of appraisal, barter exchanges involving produce become effective only when both parties involved perform a *kinyan meshikhah*. Given these facts, a barter exchange of produce is always categorized as a *sales* transaction and hence is subject to *ona'ah* regulation.[62]

(d) When a transaction is contracted through an agent and the agent is victimized by *ona'ah*, the principal is conferred nullification rights even when the amount of *ona'ah* involved is merely third degree. Nullification rights for the principal here proceed from the fact that the legitimacy of an agreement concluded through an agent derives from the presumption that power of attorney (*shelichut*) was in effect when the transaction was consummated. Given the financial loss an *ona'ah* agreement imposes on the principal, the latter may protest that his agent had no authority to enter into such an agreement on his behalf. Legitimacy is given to this protest as it must be presumed that an agent is commissioned to benefit his principal and not to impair his cause (*letakunai shelachtikh velo le'avtei*). With abuse of authority on the part of his agent forming the basis of the principal's nullification rights, the latter may exercise this right even when the degree of *ona'ah* transacted on his behalf was merely third degree.[63]

(e) When a householder sells his articles of personal use, he is not liable to *ona'ah* claims.[64] Some authorities extend his immunity to even first degree *ona'ah* claims,[65] while others limit his exemption to second degree *ona'ah* claims.[66]

The privileged status of the householder here proceeds from the presumption that anyone dealing with him realizes that the latter would not dispose of his personal utensils unless he could sell them above market price.[67] The Sages extended their exemption to the householder on an unqualified basis (*lo pelug*). Hence, even if the householder was known to be pressed for cash at the time he sold his household articles, the latter, nonetheless, qualifies for the *ona'ah* exemption. Alternatively, selling one's own household articles is regarded as a degradation. Hence, even when pressed for cash, the householder, as a means of saving face, would hold out for above market price.[68]

Given the above rationalization of the householder's favored treatment against *ona'ah* claims, *Rosh* limits the exemption to instances where the buyer was aware that he was transacting with a householder. When the buyer can establish that he was unaware that the seller was a householder, the presumption that the former waives his claims against *ona'ah* is patently invalid.[69]

*Semah* would limit the above exemption to instances where the householder, himself, conducts the sale of his articles. Should the householder entrust the sale of his articles to a broker, however, the householder would be liable to *ona'ah* claims. Disposing his articles through a dealer demonstrates on the part of the householder a despairing attitude regarding his prospects of obtaining above market price for them.[70] Disputing this view, *Turei Zahav* posits that as long as the buyer was aware that he was dealing with the householder's agent, he should presume that the agent was instructed to sell only above market price. Hence, the *ona'ah* exemption of the householder remains intact in this case as well.[71]

(f) Real estate transactions are not subject to the full scope of *ona'ah* regulations. This exclusion proceeds from exegetical interpretation of the biblical source of *ona'ah*:

*And if thou sell a sale unto thy neighbor or acquirest aught of thy neighbor's hand*[72] — something that is acquired (by being passed) from hand to hand (is subject to *ona'ah* regulation), thus excluding land, which is not moveable.[73]

*Ramban* points out that insofar as a biblical interdict against *ona'ah* is mentioned explicitly in connection with real estate transactions, the exemption cited above must be taken to refer exclusively to the restitution procedure normally provided for in *ona'ah* cases. Hence, real estate transactions are subject to the prohibition against *ona'ah*, though not to its prescribed restitution procedure.[74]

The extent of the real estate exemption is a matter of dispute. *Rambam* views it as unqualified and unlimited. Regardless of the amount of *ona'ah* involved, *ona'ah* claims of the plaintiff are discarded.[75] At the other extreme stands the restrictive authority quoted by *Rif.* According to this view the exemption is limited to second degree *ona'ah* cases. Real estate transactions involving first degree *ona'ah*, however, generate nullification rights to the plaintiff.[76] *R. Tam*, representing another view, would extend the exemption even to first degree *ona'ah* cases. Nullification rights would, however, be conferred to the plaintiff when the transaction price differs from the prevailing norm by 100 %.[77] *Tosafot*, expressing still another view, would not allow the plaintiff to void the sale unless the variance was *greater* than 100 %.[78]

Articles assimilated to real estate by means of a *hekkesh* are also free from *ona'ah* regulation. Hence, slave transactions are not subject to the laws of *ona'ah*.[79] Since Judaic law regards a worker in a sense "sold" to his employer for the duration of his contract, the labor market in general is not subject to *ona'ah* regulation. Hence, wage agreements departing from the prevailing norm are not subject to modification on account of *ona'ah*.[80] *Rambam*, however, limits the above exemption to the wage agreements of day-laborers (*po'eil*). The wage contracts of piece workers (*kablan*) do fall within the scope of *ona'ah* regulation.[81] *Ramban*, quoting some authorities, assimilates the piece worker to the day-laborer in regard to the *ona'ah* exemption.[82]

(g) Financial assets are not subject to *ona'ah* regulation. This exemption follows from exegetical interpretation of the term "sale" that appears in reference to the biblical source of the *ona'ah* prohibition cited above. The term "sale" is taken to imply that which is intrinisically sold and intrinsically bought, excluding financial assets which are not intrinsically sold or bought and exist only as evidence.[83]

FREEDOM OF ENTRY — AN HALAKHIC VIEW

One essential requirement for the efficient working of the free enterprise economy is freedom of entry. New entry and the prospect of new entry intensifies the competitive forces in the marketplace and exerts a downward pressure on price. Artificial barriers to free entry, on the other hand, generate entropy-like forces into the marketplace and are decidely injurious to consumers as price is raised artificially above what it otherwise might be.

To what extent halakha allows freedom of entry involves a discussion of the recognized rights of the community, the neighborhood and the firm to restrict or otherwise control the location of economic activity.

## THE COMMUNITY'S POWER TO CONTROL ECONOMIC ACTIVITY

The community as a collective may deny a non-resident the right to set up a business enterprise within its environs.[84]

*Levush Mordekhai* views the above communal prerogative as an economic security measure, protecting itself from foreign encroachment upon its livelihood. The established members of the community are regarded as generating the economic activity of their town. Since these individuals fully anticipate realizing the gains of their town's income-producing activities, foreign businessmen may not penetrate the town without prior communal consent.[85] What follows as a corollary is that an individual may not be denied access to a town when his purpose of entry is not to compete with local vendors but merely to assume the role of a consumer. The foreigner's entry as a consumer is guaranteed, notwithstanding the possibility that his spending activities might bid up local prices.[86]

Under normal[87] circumstances, the ability of the community to impose artificial barriers against free entry is quite limited. An examination of the restrictions placed on the community's authority in this matter bears this out.

*Rosh* posits that the power of the community to block new entry is restricted to the instance where the applicant desires to conduct business activities in the town but insists on maintaining his residence elsewhere. Should he apply for both a residency and business permit, his entry into the town may not be blocked, as the established members of the community may not claim any pre-emptive settlement rights.[88]

Other *Rishonim* dispute *Rosh*'s ruling and would allow the community the power to deny a business license to an outsider even when the latter offers to establish his residence as well as his business in the town.[89]

All the above disputants would agree, however, that current participation in the town's tax rolls confers an automatic business license to the taxpayer, despite his failure to maintain local residence.[90] Whether the community is obliged to acquiesce to a nontaxpaying outsider's offer to share in the future tax payments of the town, in exchange for a business license there, is a matter of dispute. *Rashi* would allow a rival already established in the town to require the outsider to attain town membership, i.e., rent an apartment in the town, as a prior condition to accepting his offer. *R. Tam* rules, however, that the outsider's offer must be accepted at face value. Competing firms already established in the town may not impose additional conditions on the prospective newcomer.[91]

Nonparticipation in local taxes does not always provide the community with legitimate grounds for excluding non-residents from conducting business activities in their town.

### COMPETITION IN THE FIELD OF TORAH EDUCATION

Primary school religious teachers (*melamdei tinokot*) are offered access to any community they might desire to enter. The free movement of the primary school teacher is guaranteed even when he desires to enter a town where a competitor is firmly entrenched. Competition in this profession is very favorably viewed. The Talmud's approving attitude toward rivalry here finds expression in the adage, *kinat soferim tarbeh chokhmah* (jealousy among scholars increases wisdom).[92]

According to *Sho'el Umeishiv*, freedom of movement for instructors of Mishnah and Talmud follows from the above argument with equal force. Indeed, an even more fundamental basis for guaranteeing the latter group freedom of movement is advanced by him. Compensation for teaching Mishnah and Talmud is prohibited.[93] Payment for such instruction is justified only as an opportunity cost payment, i.e., as an inducement not to seek employment elsewhere.[94] New entry in the secondary school sector therefore does not *directly* reduce the livelihood of the established teacher. Assuming that the salary of the entrenched teacher was equal to his foregone earnings, any reduction of these earnings occasioned by the new entrant merely imposes on the former a loss in the form of an opportunity cost, i.e., *income he could have earned* had he spent his time outside the secondary educational field. Now, preventing someone from earning his livelihood incurs liability only when the loss in earnings can be *directly traced* to the action of the offender. Locking someone in his home, thereby preventing him from going to work, qualifies as such a direct action. When the link between the plaintiff's loss in earnings and the action of the offender is not direct no liability is incurred.[95] Insofar as the new entrant in no way initiated any action that prevented the established teacher from earning income *outside* the secondary educational field, the former has no legal claim against the new entrant.[96]

*Chatam Sofer* would extend freedom of movement to any religious ministrant, provided that the resulting competition would produce as salubrious a result as primary-school teacher rivalry.[97]

COMPETITION WITH OUT-OF-TOWN MERCHANTS

The community's power to regulate commerce carried out by foreigners is confined to the retail trade level. No restrictions may however by placed on foreign wholesale trade activities.[98] Allowing the community to regulate foreign wholesale trade would in effect disrupt inter-community trade.[99]

The community's prerogative to regulate foreign retail trade is also not absolute. Restrictions in this area must be suspended on "market days" (*yoma deshuka*).[100] On these occasions the market-place expands to include consumers from nearby towns as well as the local population. Given that foreign retail trade at this time cannot be said as a matter of certainty to attract local customers away from local merchants,[101] *Tosafot* and *Rosh* would allow the foreign merchants to cater to the non-local portion of the market on these days.[102] A still broader view of the trading rights of foreign merchants on market days is taken by *Bet Yosef*. According to his view, foreign merchants on these days may sell their wares indiscriminately, to local and non-local customers alike.[103] The presumptive claim of local merchants to the local market is, according to *Bet Yosef*, apparently lost entirely on market days.

Retail trading privileges on these days allow foreign merchants only to sell their wares in the marketplace. Peddling their merchandise from door to door in the local community is a privilege not extended to them even on market days.[104]

Should locally available merchandise be offered by foreign merchants at a lower price, the latter group, according to *R. Yosef ha-Levi*, may not be barred from competing for local patronage. Insofar as competition here decidedly benefits local consumers, protectionist pleas of local merchants must be resisted.[105]

Citing the following Talmudic passage in Baba Metzia 60a, *Ramban* disagrees with the above ruling of *R. Yosef ha-Levi*:

> R. Judah said: Nor may he reduce the price; but the Sages say, he is to be remembered for good. What is the Rabbis' reason? Because he lowers market price.

Though the Sages regard price cutting as a fair business tactic, they would not permit a non-taxpaying outsider to employ this stratagem as a means of gaining entry into the town. How can such vendors be permitted to generate losses to local merchants? If the townspeople feel that local prices are too high, legitimate means to reduce them are readily available. Encouraging local merchants to compete with the high-priced local vendors would be one approach. Alternatively, price reductions could be mandated directly through the legislative process. Given that the community has the power to fix local prices, this body may not allow foreign merchants to effectively usurp this function by causing local prices to go down. Furthermore, argues *Ramban*, should foreign merchants be guaranteed entry whenever they offer to undersell the local competition, the community would never be able to block foreign entry. This follows from the fact that an increase in supply, *ceteris parabus*, will always exert a downard pressure on the price. Hence, regardless of whether foreign merchants initially offer to undersell local vendors, their competitive presence will nonetheless force local prices down.[106]

Should the foreign vendors offer for sale merchandise otherwise unobtainable or market wares superior to what is available locally, the community may not obstruct their entry. Heterogeneity of product, in *Bet Yosef*'s view, is what is crucial in generating free trading rights. Hence, even if the product marketed by the foreign merchant is inferior to what is available locally, the outsider's freedom of entry is vouchsafed.[107]

Debt or loan connections with members of the local community provide the foreign merchant with another legitimate basis for gaining business entry to a town. Until such time that the foreign merchant collects or pays off his debts, as the case may be, the community may not interfere with his subsistence generating business activities.[108] Though not a *bona fide* member of the community, the foreign merchant must participate in some measure in the burden of local taxation for the duration of his stay. His tax liability is assessed proportional to the volume of his business profits.

Individuals forced to leave their own communities to avoid impending harm, may enter another community on the same terms outlined above.[109]

By virtue of a special enactment of Ezra, foreign cosmetic salesmen are conferred special status. To afford women easy access to beautification aids, the community must allow these salesmen to peddle their wares from door to door. These foreign peddlers may however be prevented from marketing their wares in a retail outlet. When the peddler is a Rabbinical scholar, the latter privilege must be extended to him as well.[110]

COMPETITION WITH RABBINICAL SCHOLARS

Rabbinical scholars must be afforded by the community special treatment when they conduct commercial activities. The special treatment consists of disallowing competing firms to offer their wares on the market until the

Rabbinical scholar has managed to sell out his inventory. This courtesy is extended even to a visiting Rabbinical scholar.[111] *Ramah* and *Ri MiGash* would limit the community's obligation in this matter to the instance where the product line of the Rabbinical scholar is dominated by its local members. Should the competing sellers consist mainly of non-Jews, the above courtesy need not be extended, as delaying the arrival of local merchants to the market-place would, in any case, not eliminate from the scene the presence of competing firms.[112]

Why Rabbinical scholars are conferred special trading rights is a matter of dispute. *Rambam* posits that the courtesy proceeds from the biblical obligation to confer honor to Rabbinical scholars.[113] *Rosh*, however, views the measure as a means of minimizing time lost from Torah study. Rabbinical scholars, in contrast to their commercial competitors, normally spend their time in Torah study. Extending the Rabbinical scholar a preemptive selling right allows him to minimize the time he must devote toward earning a live-lihood, thereby maximizing the time he spends on Torah study. This arrange-ment therefore minimizes the social opportunity cost of commercial activity.[114]

THE NEIGHBORHOOD'S POWER TO CONTROL THE LOCATION OF ECONOMIC ACTIVITY

A resident of a dwelling facing a courtyard shared by other residents may be restrained by any one of his neighbors from conducting traffic-generating activities. Examples of such activities, cited in the Talmud, include the establishment of a weaving concern, a blood-letting enterprise and a Trade School.[115] Moreover, residents of the courtyard may restrain each other from selling or renting their apartments to professionals of the types men-tioned above.[116]

The residents of a courtyard may not restrain one of their members from establishing a Torah school in his premises, notwithstanding the negative ex-ternality (unintentional, incidental harm) his enterprise would impose on them. Between the conflicting interests of upholding the amenity rights of residents of the courtyard and allowing Torah education to proceed unhindered, the latter is judged to be more important. Establishing a religious school pro-motes the viability of Torah education and is consistent with the intent of R. Joshua ben Gamala's ancient ordinance requiring local communities to maintain religious educational institutions for the young.[117]

Should the class size of the Torah school exceed the maximum level of fifty[118] prescribed by the original ordinance of R. Joshua ben Gamala,[119] any resident of the courtyard may, according to *Rashi*, obtain a restraining order to halt the enterprise.[120] Other *Poskim* (codifiers of Jewish law) disagree. The activity remains one of religious character, notwithstanding its improper structure, and therefore may not be halted by means of a restraining order.[121]

*Tur* assimilates any enterprise of a religious purpose with Torah education. Hence, a restraining order would not be issued to halt any enterprise of a religious character.[122] *Rashi* and *Ramban*, however, confine unhindered status to Torah education enterprises exclusively. Any other traffic-generating activity, despite its religious purpose, may be restrained by any resident of the courtyard.[123]

Traffic congestion generates two distinct annoyances to the residents of the courtyard, namely noise and time delay. *Rashba* posits that noise generating activities alone do not provide adequate grounds for the issuance of a restraining order. Time delay as a consequence of the traffic congestion is what provides the residents with a legitimate basis for obtaining a restraining order. Hence, should a resident of the courtyard desire to carry out in his premises noise-generating activities not involving traffic congestion, i.e., hammering and grinding activities, complaining residents are denied a restraining order.[124]

*Rambam* and *Rabbenu Yerucham*, however, regard noise-generating activities alone as adequate grounds for the issuance of a restraining order.[125] Noise externalities, according to this school of thought, are classified into two categories, those involving traffic congestion and those not involving the latter nuisance. In the former instance, a restraining order is issued at the request of any resident of the courtyard even if the activity had previously gone unprotested for an interval normally sufficient to establish a *chazakah*[126] privilege for the perpetrator. *Chazakah* does not fortify the rights of the violator as the nuisance itself, time delay, cannot be directly linked to his, the violator's, actions. Moreover, traffic congestion occurring on a particular day is independent of traffic congestion occurring on another day. With each instance of time delay treated as a new and independent event, a request by a resident of the courtyard for a restraining order is honored at any time, despite his previous lack of protest.

In sharp contrast, noise externalities not involving traffic congestion are linked directly to the actions of the perpetrator and are therefore properly regarded as his continuous action. Hence, should the residents have allowed the noise externality to go on unprotested, *chazakah*, in this instance, does fortify the violator's right to continue this enterprise.[127]

A resident of a dwelling of a closed alley, according to *Rambam*, enjoys the same rights to halt externality-generating activities of his neighbors as does the resident of a courtyard. Though not entirely free from public traffic as it is open to a street from one side, the closed alley, nonetheless, encounters much less traffic than a public thoroughfare. Given the relative quiet the closed alley normally enjoys, residents may prevent each other from initiating enterprises that would tend to increase the flow of traffic.[128] Should the residents of the closed alley allow one of its members to engage in a traffic-generating enterprise, they forfeit thereby any concurrent right to oppose the entry of a member of another closed alley desiring to engage in the same activity. Protestations by the members of the closed alley that they are only willing to tolerate an increase in traffic when it is generated by one of their own members, but not when a newcomer is the cause of this added nuisance, is denied.[129]

Disputing *Rambam*'s view, *Tosafot, Nemukei Yosef, Ramban* and *Rif* would not confer restraining order rights to members of a closed alley. Insofar as a closed alley is in any case subject to a traffic flow, its members may not restrain each other from engaging in traffic-generating enterprises.[130]

### RIGHTS OF INDIVIDUAL FIRMS TO RESTRICT COMPETITION

Subject to the power of the neighborhood to protect itself against externality-generating activities, a *bona fide* member of the community is guaranteed unlimited business access of the town. Hence, a firm may not be restrained by a competing firm from locating even in close proximity to it.[131]

The taxpaying non-resident may, however, be prevented by his local rival from entering the closed alley from which he conducts his enterprise. Any other closed alley is open to the taxpaying non-resident, provided, of course, his neighbors are willing to tolerate the externalities involved in his enterprise.[132]

When the profits of the original monopolist are not merely reduced but his livelihood ruined as a result of new entry, the entrenched firm, according to *Chatam Sofer*, is entitled to monopoly status.

What leads *Chatam Sofer* to this unusual ruling is an attempt to reconcile conflicting rabbinic opinion in Baba Batra 21b regarding the right of an established firm to restrict free entry. R. Huna would confer on an established firm monopoly status in the closed alley of its location, while R. Huna ben R. Joshua would allow a rival to locate even in close proximity to an established firm. *Chatam Sofer* posits that the above disputants are in basic agreement as each refers to a different case. R. Huna's protectionist philosophy is restricted to instances where the effect of new entry would ruin, not merely reduce, the livelihood of the established firm. The free entry advocacy of R. Huna ben R. Joshua, on the other hand, is confined to instances where the effect of the new entry would be merely to reduce the profit margin of the entrenched competitor and not to deprive him of his livelihood entirely. That R. Huna's view is not discarded in favor of R. Huna ben Joshua's view is bolstered by the fact that several rulings of the *Rishonim* follow the protectionist line of reasoning of R. Huna. Foremost of these rulings is the decision of *Aviasaf*, quoted in *Bet Yosef*. This Rabbi confers monopoly status to a store located at the extreme end of a closed alley. Allowing another firm to locate immediately in front of the established firm would effectively ruin the livelihood of the original competitor as passersby would be blocked from its view and take all their business to the new entrant.

Another rabbi who follows a protectionist philosophy is *Ri MiGash*. His protectionist advocacy is clearly seen by his comments on the following Talmudic passage in Baba Batra 21b:

> May we say that this view (R. Huna's) is supported by the following: Fishing nets must be kept away from (the hiding place of) a fish (which has been spotted by another fisherman) the full length of the fish's swim! And how much is this? Rabbah son of R. Huna says: A *parasang*? — fish are different because they look about (for food).

Why a fisherman is conferred a territorial preserve, while a tradesman is not similarly treated, is explained by *Ri MiGash* as follows: A fisherman's design to capture a large fish he sights is effectively frustrated when another fisherman places his net between this fish's hiding place and the bait. The latter's action has the effect of intercepting the swarm of little fish that surround the large fish. Insofar as the large fish will change direction as soon as he notices that the small fish have been caught, the action of the intruder effectively deprives the first fisherman of his catch. In contrast, the arrival of a new firm on the competitive scene in no way *forces* customers to discontinue their patronage of the entrenched firm. With new entry generating no deprivation effects on the established firm, the latter is denied a territorial monopoly.[133]

*Igrot Moshe* concurs with the protectionist philosophy espoused by *Chatam Sofer*.[134] Nonetheless, a large number of *Poskim* do not regard *deprivation of livelihood alone* as valid grounds for conferring a territorial monopoly.[135]

The anti-protectionist school views the talmudic dispute, cited above, as irreconcilable and rules in accordance with the free entry advocacy of R. Huna ben R. Joshua. *Aviasaf*'s view is regarded as being rooted in the protectionist philosophy of R. Huna and therefore not consonant with mainstream thought. Similarly, *Ri MiGash*'s explanation of the preserve rights of fishermen must be regarded as expressing a minority viewpoint as it is not in conformity with the mainstream interpretation of this right offered by *Rashi* and *Rambam ad locum*. What qualifies the first fisherman for a territorial preserve, according to *Rashi* in Baba Batra 21b, is not the deprivation effects of the interloper's action, as *Ri MiGash* would have it, but rather the *anticipation of gain* he enjoyed prior to the arrival of the rival. Casting bait in the fish's hiding place assures the fisherman that he will be able to lure fish into his net. With his catch thereby assured, another fisherman may not spread his net at the same spot, as doing so would deprive the former of an *anticipated* gain. In contrast, a firm may locate in close proximity to another firm, as the entrenched competitor was never *guaranteed* a clientele. Each firm sets up shop in its own premises and customers decide to patronize the firm of their choice.

*Chelkat Yaakov*, elaborating on *Rashi*'s view, maintains that even if the original firm was the only firm of its kind in the entire town prior to the arrival of the new entrant, nevertheless, the former monopolist's clientele cannot be regarded as guaranteed. This follows from the fact that the original firm, even in R. Huna's view, could not prevent a competing firm from locating in an adjacent closed alley. Hence, his clientele could have, at any time, been lured away to a distant competitor. In contrast, casting bait at a safe distance from the first fisherman would in no way affect the latter's catch. Casting bait in a particular location, therefore, establishes for the fisherman a territorial preserve.

Another difference between the cases, according to *Chelkat Yaakov*, is that the anticipated gain of the fisherman, the catch of fish, is existent at the time the intruder arrives at the scene. In contrast, the anticipated gain of the storekeeper, the patronage of his long-standing clientele, is non existent (*devar shelo ba la'olam*) at the time the rival competitor sets up shop. With the anticipated gain in the latter case non existent at the time of the intrusion, the entrenched competitor is denied the right to treat his former clientele as his exclusive preserve.[136]

*Ramban, ad locum,* offers a different rationale for the preserve rights of the fisherman. What the second fisherman is prohibited from doing is to spread his net in close vicinity to the net of the first fisherman as such action could result in directly depriving the former of what is rightfully his. Fish already captured in the first fisherman's net could, at times, spring out into the second fisherman's net. With only this fear accounting for the privileged status of the first fisherman, an entrenched competitor does not qualify for similar treatment unless his degree of anticipation of gain parallels the confidence level of the first fisherman. Such parallelism, obviously, cannot be demonstrated by the monopolist tradesman in presenting his case against the interloper.

With anticipation of gain, according to both *Rashi* and *Ramban,* providing the basis for generating preserve rights for the fisherman, the tradesman qualifies for the privilege too when his degree of anticipation of gain parallels that of the original fisherman. Such parallelism occurs, in *Chatam Sofer*'s view, when a vendor and his customer reach agreement regarding price and are ready to consummate their transaction with a *kinyan.* At this point, a competing vendor may not interfere with the imminent sale. Interfering with the sale at this point deprives the would-be seller of an anticipated gain equivalent to the anticipated gain of the original fisherman.[137]

Another circumstance apparently analogous to the fisherman case occurs when an individual enjoys a long-standing franchise right with a gentile nobleman to purchase merchandise from him or to engage in a commercial venture that requires his approval (*maiarupea*). With the franchiser anticipating renewal of the long-standing relationship, may another individual persuade the nobleman to transfer the franchise to him? *Rema*[138] quotes conflicting opinions on this matter. Some authorities prohibit the action, while others permit it. Noting that the degree of anticipation of gain needed to qualify for an exclusive privilege is of greater magnitude according to *Ramban* compared to *Rashi, Chatam Sofer* posits that the franchiser's degree of anticipation of gain meets *Rashi*'s criterion but falls short of *Ramban*'s criterion to earn an exclusive privilege. The conflicting views quoted in *Rema* on this matter are therefore rooted in the controversy between *Rashi* and *Ramban.*[139]

*Chatam Sofer* would confer monopoly status on publishers of Talmud and *Rishonim*. Given the decreasing-cost nature of the industry along with the elastic demand it faces, profits are predicated on the ability of publishers to sell their books in large quantities. Allowing unbridled competition in this industry would thus increase the risk factor and reduce the profit motive. With the wide dissemination of essential religious books endangered by competitive forces, a legitimate basis for conferring monopoly status is established.[140]

Equity in the treatment of market participants demands that the buyer, too, be protected against interference when his degree of anticipation of acquisition reaches a certain level. This level occurs when negotiations between him and the seller advance to the stage just prior to *kinyan*. At this point, a third party may not step in and offer to purchase the product at hand. The position of the buyer at this point is metaphorically compared to a poor person moving about a stack, anxiously waiting for its removal in anticipation of picking up a forgotten sheaf (*ani hamehapekh bechararah*). Interference at this point brands the offender a wicked person (*rasha*). Nonetheless, halakha does not go so far as to void the purchase of the interloper in order to allow the original purchaser realization of his anticipated acquisition.[141]

With degree of anticipation of gain forming the basis of both the fisherman's preserve rights, as discussed above, and the buyer's right to protection against interference, the asymmetrical halakhic treatment of these two cases requires explanation. Why is the fisherman protected to the extent that he has a legal claim to the catch of fish that was snatched away from him, while the frustrated buyer is not empowered to void the transaction concluded by the interloper? The critical difference between the two cases, according to *Masat Binyamin*, is that in the former instance the anticipated gain constitutes the plaintiff's source of livelihood (*umanuto bekhakh*), while in the latter case the anticipated gain cannot be similarly classified, as *everyone* assumes the role of consumer. Legal claim to the anticipated gain exists only when the gain is a source of livelihood. When the latter condition is not fulfilled, the interloper is branded a wicked person; nonetheless, halakha does not go so far as to void the transaction concluded by the latter.[142]

*Rashi* extends the interdict against interference to cases involving the acquisition of a windfall gain. Hence, should an individual find someone poised to take possession of public property (*hefker*), he may not pounce upon the object and anticipate the former in performing the *kinyan* necessary to acquire legal possession of it. Disputing *Rashi*'s view, *R. Tam* posits that the above interdict does not apply to windfall gains. Interference is prohibited only when the offender would have easily obtained the object at hand elsewhere. With this obviously not the case in regard to windfall gains, interference prior to the point when legal possession takes place is not prohibited.[143]

*Rema* rules in accordance with *R. Tam*.[144] This leads some authorities to suspend the interdict against interference in sales transactions when the object involved is a *bargain*.[145] *Ramban*,[146] quoted in *Shakh, ad locum*, however posits that the interdict against interference in sales transactions is unqualified and applies to bargain sales as well.

Though halakha takes a neutral stand in regard to the act of snatching away someone's anticipated windfall gain, the following exception to this rule, recorded in Gittin 59b, should be noted. Here, we are told that when a person climbs to the top of an olive tree to glean *shikcha*, or *leket*, the fruit that falls to the ground, though not legally the possession of the poor man, is regarded as the latter's exclusive preserve. Should another poor man anticipate the first poor man in performing the necessary *kinyan* to acquire possession of this fruit, this act is regarded as robbery by Rabbinical enactment (*gezel midivreihem*). Nonetheless, halakha does not go so far as to force the offender to return the gleanings to the first poor man. Why this case is set apart from other instances involving acquisition from public property is explained by *Masat Binyamin* as stemming from the heightened level of anticipation of acquisition the poor man experiences as a result of his feat of *removing* the gleanings from their original place on the top of the tree. Snatching away his anticipated gain at this point is, however, not regarded as outright theft as the anticipated gain is not considered a normal source of livelihood. Though a poor man is preoccupied in collecting forgotten sheafs, he presumably abhors his status and looks forward to the day he will become gainfully employed.[147]

# NOTES

1. For classical treatments of the optimizing-producing results of the free enterprise system c. f. Adam Smith, *The Wealth of Nations* (London: Routledge, 1913); John Stuart Mill, *Principles of Political Economy* (London: Longmans, Green, 1926); and Milton Friedman, *Capitalism and Freedom* (Chicago: University of Chicago Press, 1962).

2. For a treatment of collectives from a halakhic perspective, within a historical framework, v. Simon Federbush, *The Jewish Concept of Labor* (Torah Culture Department of the Jewish Agency and Hapoel Hamizrachi of America, 1956), pp. 7–16.

3. Resp. *Rashba*, Vol. 1, no. 729; vol. 3, no. 411; vol. 4, nos. 142, 311; vol. 5, no. 126; Resp. *Rabbenu Gershom Me'or ha-Gola*, no. 67; Resp. *Maharam* of Rothenbrug, ed. Lemberg, no. 423; Resp. *Yakhin u-Vo'az*, ed. Eidelberg, pt. 2, no. 2.

4. Resp. *Rashba*, Vol. 3, no. 411; Resp. *Ribash*, no. 399; Resp. *Maharam Alashkar*, no. 49; *Tashbez* 2:132.

5. B.B. 8b.

6. Resp. *Mabit*, Vol. 1, no. 237.

7. *Ibid.*

8. *Tur*, Choshen Mishpat 231:28.

9. The one-sixth profit rate limitation is understood by Sh. Ar. *HoRav* (Hilkhot Midot Umishkalot) as a *shethuth mil'bar*, as opposed to a *shethuth mil'gav*.

10. V.B.B. 90a; *Rosh* B.B. V: 28; *Tur*, op. cit.; *Yad*, Hilkhot Mechirah XIV:1; Sh. Ar. Choshen Mishpat 231:20.

11. *Maggid Mishnah*, *Yad*, Hilkhot Mechirah XIV:2.

12. *Bet Yosef*, Tur, op. cit. 23:28.

13. *Semah*, Sh. Ar., op. cit., note 36.

14. Beraita B. M. 51b; *Rosh* B.M. IV:19; *Yad*, op. cit., XIII:6; *Tur*, op. cit., 227:39; Sh. Ar., op. cit., 227:28.

15. *Meiri*, B.M. 40b; *Rosh* B.M. III:16; *Tur*, op. cit., 231:26 and comment of *Pereshah* ad locum. The implicit wage element of the cost base is presumably limited to the competitive rate for the type of work performed.

16. *Rosh*, op. cit.; *Tur*, op. cit.

17. *Rashbam* B.B. 90a; *Rabbeinu Shimshon* quoted in *Hagahot Maimoniyot*, Hilkhot Mechirah XII:1; *Bach*, Tur, op. cit., 231:26 understand this to be *Rambam*'s view also.

18. *Rosh*, B.B. V:28; *Tur*, op. cit., 231:26; Sh. Ar., op. cit., 231:20.

19. *Tur*, op. cit.; Sh. Ar., op. cit.

20. *Tur*, op. cit.

21. Sh. Ar., op. cit., 231:24. For an interesting glimpse into how the Sages viewed the effect of hoarding on market price v. B.B. 90b.

22. B.B. 91a; *Yad*, op. cit., XIV:4; Sh. Ar., op. cit., 231:23.

23. *Rashbam*, B.B. 91a; *Arukh Hashulchan*, op. cit., 231:23.

24. B.B. 90a; *Yad*, op. cit., XIV:8; Sh. Ar., op. cit., 231:26.

25. *Yad*, op. cit.; Sh. Ar., op. cit.

26. R. Simeon b. Gamliel here relied on the principle *eth la'asoth la'Shem, heferu thorathecha* (v. Tifereth Yisroel, ad locum).

27. Resp. *Zemach Zedek* (Krochmal), no. 28.

28. *Rashi*, Ta'anith 10a, 15b; *Tur*, Orach Chaim 572:1; *Magen Avraham*, Sh. Ar. Orach Chaim, 572:1.

29. Sh. Ar. Choshen Mishpat, 228.

30. V. Sh. Ar., op. cit. 228.

31. V. Sh. Ar., op. cit., 227.

32. V. Sh. Ar., op. cit., 232, 233, 234.

33. V. Sh. Ar., op. cit., 220.

34. V. B. M. 61a; *Tur*, Choshen Mishpat, 227:1; *Semah*, Sh. Ar., op. cit., 227 note 1.

35. B. M. 50b; *Yad*, op. cit., XII:4; *Rosh* B. M. IV:15; *Tur*, op. cit., 227:6; Sh. Ar., op. cit., 227:4.

36. Sh. Ar., op. cit.; *Yad*, op. cit.

37. *Rosh* (B. B. V:14) understands this to be the view of *Rif.*

38. Quoted in *Rosh* B. B. V:14; also quoted in *Ran* B. B. 84a and *Rema*, Sh. Ar., op. cit., 227:4.

39. B. M. 50b; *Rosh* B. M. IV:15; *Yad*, op. cit., XII:2; *Tur*, op. cit., 227:3; Sh. Ar., op. cit., 227:2.

40. B. M. 50b; *Rosh*, op. cit.; *Yad*, op. cit., XIII:3; *Tur*, op. cit., 227:4; Sh. Ar., op. cit.

41. B. M. IV:20.

42. Viewing the above presumption as being universally descriptive of human nature, *Semah* (Sh. Ar., op. cit., note 14) rules that even if the plaintiff had not yet made payment, consummation of the transaction by means of *kinyan* obligates the latter to make payment in full, including the *ona'ah* component of the sale price. The plaintiff's protest that he does not waive his claim against third degree *ona'ah* is received incredulously, as *everyone* is presumed to waive his claims against third degree *ona'ah* (*batlah daato eitzel kol adam*). The above presumption is viewed in a different light by *Machaneh Ephraim* (Hilkhot *ona'ah* chap. 13). In his view the presumption is merely descriptive of majority behavior. Viewing the presumption in this attenuated form effectively places the claimant at a disadvantage. Hence, in the event payment had already been made, the plaintiff's demand for restoration of the third degree *ona'ah* is denied as we presume the latter is of the majority that waives such such claims. On the other hand, in the event payment was not yet made, the buyer need not pay the *ona'ah* component of the purchase price, as the latter may insist that he is of the minority that does not waive such claims.

43. *Yad*, op. cit.; *Tur*, op. cit.; Sh. Ar., op. cit.

44. Commentary on Leviticus XXV:14.

45. *Sefer Hachinuch*, Mitzvah 337.

46. *Arukh Hashulchan*, op. cit., 227:7.

47. B. M. 51a; *Rosh* B. M. IV:17; *Yad*, op. cit., XII:8; *Tur*, op. cit., 227:13; Sh. Ar., op. cit., 227:14.

48. B. M. 49b; *Rosh* B. M. IV:15; *Yad*, op. cit., XII:5; *Tur*, op. cit., 227:15; Sh. Ar., op. cit., 227:7.

49. *Rashi*, B. M. 49b.

50. *Arukh Hashulchan*, op. cit., 227:10.

51. V. B. M. 50b; *Yad*, op. cit., XII:6, 7; *Tur*, op. cit., 227:10, Sh. Ar., op. cit., 227:8.

52. *Rema*, op. cit., 227:7 quoting *Mordekhai* (B. M. IV:307); *Tur Zahavei* ad locum;

*Nitivot Hamishpat* note 4; *Arukh Hashulchan*, op. cit., 227:9. For a variant interpretation of *Mordekhai* v. *Semah* and *Ketzot* ad locum.

53. *Ritva*, Kiddushin 8b. Ruling of *Ritva*, as pointed out by *Ketzot* (Sh. Ar., op. cit., 227, note 1) and *Machaneh Ephraim* (Hilkhot *ona'ah* chap. 20) appears to follow R. Judah's line of reasoning in Baba Metzia 58b. Since the halakha rests with the Sages, *Ritva*'s position appears enigmatic. For a reconciliation of *Ritva*'s ruling with the majority view of the Sages v. Rabbi Aaron Walkin's commentary on *Yereim* (*Saviv LiYereav*) 259:4.

54. *Yad*, op. cit., XIII:3, 4; *Tur*, op. cit., 227:26; Sh. Ar., op. cit., 227:21.

55. V. Kiddushin 19b; V. Sh. Ar., Even HaEzer 38.

56. *Yad*, op. cit.; *Tur*, op. cit.; Sh. Ar., Choshen Mishpat 227:21.

57. B. M. 51b; *Tur*, op. cit., 227:37; Sh. Ar., op. cit., 227:27.

58. *Yad*, op. cit., XIII:5. For a variant view of what constitutes selling on trust, *Hagaot Ashri*, Baba Metzia, IV.

59. *Arukh Hashulchan*, op. cit., 227:28.

60. Leviticus XXV:12.

61. V. B. M. 47a; *Talmidei HaRashba* ad locum; *Yad*, op. cit., XIII:1; *Tur*, op. cit., 227:20. For a variant opinion v. *Ravad, Yad*, op. cit.

62. *Arukh Hashulchan*, op. cit., 227:21.

63. Kiddushin 42b; *Yad*, op. cit., XIII:9; Sh. Ar., op. cit., 227:30.

64. B. M. 51a; *Rosh* B. M. IV:16; *Yad*, op. cit., XIII:2; *Tur*, op. cit., 227:23; Sh. Ar., op. cit., 227:23.

65. *Nemukei Yosef*, B. M. IV; Sh. Ar., op. cit., 227:24.

66. *Shitah Mekubetzet* B. M. 51a; "some authorities" quoted in Sh. Ar., op. cit., 227:24.

67. *Yad*, op. cit.; *Tur*, op. cit.; Sh. Ar., op. cit.

68. *Arukh Hashulchan*, op. cit., 227:24.

69. Resp. *Rosh Kelal* 102, quoted by *Tur*, op. cit., 227:27 and Sh. Ar., op. cit., 227:23.

70. *Semah*, Sh. Ar., op. cit., note 42.

71. *Turei Zahav*, Sh. Ar., op. cit.

72. Leviticus XXV:14.

73. B. M. 56b.

74. Commentary on Leviticus XXV:14.

75. *Yad*, op. cit., XIII:8, *Shakh* (Sh. Ar., Choshen Mishpat 66:122) rules in accordance with *Rambam*.

76. B. M. 57a.

77. Quoted in *Rosh* B. M. IV:21.

78. B. M. 57a; B. K. 14b.

79. B. M. 56b; *Rosh*, op. cit.; *Yad*, op. cit.; *Tur*, op. cit., 227:40; Sh. Ar., op. cit., 227:29.

80. *Yad*, op. cit., XIII:15; *Tur*, op. cit., 227:45–46; Sh. Ar., op. cit., 227:33.

81. *Yad*, op. cit., XIII:18; *Tur*, op. cit., 227:47.

82. *Nov. Ramban*, B. M. 56b.

83. B. M. 56b; *Rosh* B. M. IV:21; *Yad*, op. cit., XIII:8; *Tur*, op. cit., 227:40; Sh. Ar., op. cit., 227:29.

84. V. B. B. 21b.

85. Nov. *Levush Mordekhai* B. B. Chap. 10.

86. *Maharik*, no. 172.
87. For halakhic points regarding the power of the community to control the location of economic activity under conditions of Galuth v. *Mordechai*, Baba Kama, X:178; Resp. *Maharik* nos. 172, 191; Resp. *Maharam* of Rothenburg, ed. Prague, no. 10001; *Darkhei Moshe, Tur*, op. cit.; 156 note 9; Resp. *Rema*, no. 52; *Rema*, Sh. Ar., op. cit., 156:7; *Semah*, Sh. Ar., op. cit., 156, note 28.
88. Quoted by *Tur*, op. cit., 156:15, also quoted by *Rema*, op. cit., 156:7.
89. *Maharik* (*Shoresh* 191) interprets this to be the view of *Rashi, Rabbenu Tam* and *Ramban*; *Rema*, op. cit.; *be'ur HaGra*, ad locum; Resp. *Rema*, no. 46.
90. B. B. 21b; *Yad*, Hilkhot Shekheinim VI:8; *Tur*, op. cit., 156:11; Sh. Ar., op. cit., 156:5.
91. Quoted by *Hagaot Ashri* B. B. II:12; v. *Bet Yosef*, op. cit.
92. *Raavan* B. B. 29b; *Bet Yosef*, op. cit.; *Derisha*, ad locum note 13. For a variant view v. *Tosafot* B. B. 21b.
93. V. Nedraim 37a.
94. V. *Tosafot* Bekhorot 29a.
95. Sh. Ar., op. cit., 420:11.
96. *Shoel Umeishiv*, 4th ed., vol. I, no. 13.
97. Resp., Choshen Mishpat no. 79.
98. *Rosh*, B. B. II:12; *Tur*, op. cit., 156:11; Sh. Ar., op. cit., 156:7.
99. *Bet Yosef*, op. cit., 156:11.
100. B. B. 22a; *Rosh* B. B., op. cit.; *Yad*, op. cit., VI:10; *Tur*, op. cit.; Sh. Ar., op. cit., 156:7. *Bach*, ad locum, understands *yoma deshuka* to refer to the weekly market days and not to the elaborate annual fairs. For a variant interpretation of *yoma deshuka* v. *Arukh Hashulchan*, op. cit., 156:10.
101. *Bet Yosef*, op. cit.
102. *Tosafot* B. B. 22a; *Rosh*, op. cit.
103. *Bet Yosef*, op. cit.
104. B. B. 22a; *Rosh*, op. cit.; *Yad*, op. cit.; *Tur*, op. cit.; Sh. Ar., op. cit.
105. Quoted in *Bet Yosef*, op. cit.
106. Nov. *Ramban* B. B. 22a.
107. *Bet Yosef*, op. cit.
108. *Rambam* (*Yad*, op. cit., VI:10) understands the phrase *It lan ashira'ei* in B. B. 22a to mean that the foreign merchants were conferred commercial privileges because they were debtors to members of the local community. *Tur* (op. cit., 156:11) interprets the phrase as meaning that the foreign merchants attained their privileged status on the basis of being creditors to members of the local community.
109. *Bet Yosef*, op. cit.
110. B. B. 22a; *Rosh*, op. cit.; *Yad*, op. cit., VI:9; *Tur*, op. cit., 156:12; Sh. Ar., op. cit., 156:6.
111. B. B. 22a; *Rosh* B. B. II:13; *Yad*, Hilkhot Talmud Torah, VI:10; *Tur*, op. cit., 156:14; *Tur*, Yoreh De'ah, 243:6; Sh. Ar., Yoreh De'ah 243:4.
112. Quoted by *Tur*, Choshen Mishpat, 156:14; also quoted by Sh. Ar., Yoreh De'ah, op. cit.
113. Commentary on Aboth IV:4.

114. B. B. II:13. For practical differences in halakha proceeding from the dispute between *Rambam* and *Rosh* v. *Einayim LaMishpat* B. B. 22a.
115. Mishnah B. B. 20b; *Rosh*, op. cit., II:12; *Tur*, op. cit.; Sh. Ar., op. cit., 156:12.
116. *Tur*, op. cit. *Mordekhai* (B.B. II:514) advances a variant opinion here. In his view, neighboring residents may interfere with only the *rental* of an apartment in the courtyard to one of these professionals. The *sale* of a home to one of these individuals may, however, not be blocked. Should the professional desire subsequently to set up his enterprise in his newly acquired home, any resident of the courtyard may, of course, at that point obtain a restraining order to halt his activity. For an explanation of *Mordekhai's* view v. *Derisha, Tur*, ad locum, note 2.
117. B. B. 21a; *Rosh*, op. cit., 12; *Yad*, op. cit., VI:11, 12; *Tur*, op. cit., 156:8; Sh. Ar., op. cit., 156:3.
118. When the number of pupils in the town exceed twenty-five, the community, according to *Rambam* (*Yad*, Hilkhot Talmud Torah II:5), is required to hire a teacher's aide to assist the teacher in his educational duties. *Rosh* (B. B. II:7) would, however, postpone the latter requirement until the pupil population reaches forty. Nonetheless, when the number of pupils in the town reaches fifty, the class must be split into two separate groups and instructed separately.
119. B. B. 21a; *Rosh*, op. cit.; *Yad*, op. cit.; *Tur*, Yoreh De'ah 245:14–16; Sh. Ar., Yoreh De'ah, 245:15.
120. B. B. 21a. The above presentation of *Rashi's* view is based on understanding of *Ramban* (Nov. B. B. 21a) and *Derisha* (*Tur*, Choshen Hamishpat, note 1). For a variant interpretation of *Rashi* v. *Bet Yosef*, ad locum.
121. *Tosafot* B. B. 21a; Nov. *Ramban*, B. B. 21a.
122. *Tur*, op. cit., 156:8.
123. B. B. 21a.
124. Nov. *Rashba* B. B. 21a. This is also view of *Ramban* ad locum.
125. V. *Yad*, Hilkhot Shekheinim VI:12; *Rabbenu Yerucham*, quoted in *Bet Yosef*, op. cit., 156.
126. A license to continue an activity by virtue of it having been carried out previously uncontested.
127. *Derisha*, op. cit., note 3; *Netivot Hamishpat*, Sh. Ar., Choshen Mishpat, 156, note 1.
128. *Yad*, op. cit., VI:5.
129. V. *Bet Yosef*, op. cit.
130. B. B. 21a.
131. *Ibid.*
132. *Rashi* and *Tosafot* on interpretation of *Bet Yosef*, op. cit.; *Tur*, op. cit., 156:10; *Rema*, op. cit., 156:5. *Rambam*, according to *Bet Yosef*, ad locum, expresses a variant view here. In the latter's view the taxpaying nonresident is conferred the same unlimited business access as the local firm.
133. Resp. *Chatam Sofer*, Choshen Mishpat, no. 78.
134. Resp. *Igrot Moshe*, Choshen Mishpat, no. 38.
135. Resp. *Beit Ephraim*, Choshen Mishpat, no. 26; Resp. *Chelkat Yaakov*, no. 65; *Einayim LaMishpat*, B. B. 21b.

136. *Chelkat Yaakov*, op. cit.
137. Resp. *Chatam Sofer*, op. cit.
138. *Rema*, op. cit., 156:7.
139. Resp. *Chatam Sofer*, op. cit. *Chelkat Yaakov* would not, in our view, link the strict opinion quoted in *Rema* with *Rashi*'s line of thought. One essential difference between the fisherman and tradesman cases, in his view, as will be recalled, is that in the former case the anticipated gain is existent at the time the intrusion occured, while in the latter case it is not. With the anticipated gain of the franchiser non-existent in nature, no grounds for conferring him an exclusive privilege exist.
140. *Ibid.*
141. V. Kiddushim 59a; *Tur*, op. cit., 237:1; Sh. Ar., op. cit., 237:1.
142. Resp. *Masat Binyamin*, no. 27.
143. Kiddushin 59b.
144. *Rema*, op. cit., 237:1.
145. *Ibid.*
146. Nov. B. B. 54b.
147. Resp. *Masat Binyamin*, op. cit.

# TORAH AND SECULAR STUDIES:
# THE HUMANITIES

LEO LEVI

## 1. Introduction

Defining the role of secular studies in Torah Judaism is a problem that has occupied the Sages of the Talmud and the later authorities — down to our own generation. But, as we probe their opinions, we note a most curious fact. We find, on the one hand, a very positive approach:

1. "Contemplate His creation, for thereby you will recognize the Creator."[1]
2. "It is a *Mitzvah* to calculate seasons and constellations ... He who knows how to calculate seasons and constellations and does not calculate them, concerning him the Verse says: 'They would not regard the acts of God, and the work of His hands they did not see.'"[2]
3. "When you contemplate and recognize all the creatures and see God's wisdom in all [of them], your love of God will increase."[3]
4. "It is a duty incumbent upon us to contemplate the creatures and the proof of the Creator's wisdom adduced therefrom."[4]
5. "All the sciences are needed for Torah study and are a ladder thereby to ascend to the divine science (theology)."[5]
6. "The other sciences are a ladder thereby to ascend to the wisdom of Torah."[6]
7. "Every one of the seven sciences* is excellent in the eyes of our Sages

*Leo Levi, Ph.D, former President of the AOJS both in Israel and the U.S.A. He is Professor of Physics at the Jerusalem College of Technology and Consultant to the National Physical Laboratory of Israel. A major part of Dr. Levi's paper appeared in Hebrew in* Torah Umada (*Vol.* 6, 45–52, 5736).

\* The "seven sciences" are[5]: "the science of logic; the science of numbers; the science of measurement; the science of nature; astronomy; the science of music; and the science of the divine."

and they loved it completely. You will not find in any *Agadah* — not in the Babylonian nor in the Jerusalem Talmud, nor in any *Midrash* — that they deprecated any science."[7]

8. "To the extent to which a person lacks knowledge in the other sciences, he will lack accordingly a hundred-fold in the science of Torah."[8]

9. "All the other sciences are entrances and gates to the Torah."[9]

On the other hand, we find expressions deprecating other studies:

1. "He who reads 'excluded books' has no share in the world to come."[10] "And the Book of Sira is also forbidden to read."[11]

2. "Cursed be he who teaches his son the 'science of Greek.'"[12]

3. "Restrain your sons from *higayon* (secular wisdom)."[13]

4. "To walk (in the words of Torah): make them primary and do not make them secondary; let your dealings be only in them; do not mingle anything else with them; do not say 'I have studied Israel's wisdom and will now go to study the wisdom of the nations'. . . "[14]

5. "Repair of the body and straightness of human conduct [is attained] by occupation with Mishnah and Talmud . . . and he who diverts his attention from these and occupies himself with [philosophy] will throw off the yoke of Torah and divine reverence . . . [and eventually] will throw off all words of the Torah completely."[15]

6. "'Why do you spend money for no bread and tire yourself for no satisfaction'. . . from here we learn that we should not occupy ourselves with other sciences, only with the main one, which is our Torah."[16]

It would seem, on first sight, that these are simply conflicting opinions, and just as our Sages disagree on other points, so do they disagree on this. But when we study the matter in greater depth, we find that there is practically no explicit disagreement on any of these points — each statement stands undisputed in its context. Furthermore, even the authorities quoted appear to contradict themselves. We cited the words of Rav Hai Gaon[15] who strongly deprecates secular studies; but elsewhere[17] he writes:* "Know mathematics and understand medical treatises." Also the Gaon of Vilna,

---

* Since the exact intention of the Gaon there is not clear, I bring here the context: "Know wisdom and if its knowledge is transcendent/know mathematics and understand medical treatises/and know the conjunction of the moon/and the time of the festivals each year."

whose words of extreme praise for the sciences we quoted above[8], wrote elsewhere[18] concerning Maimonides (RaMBaM): "He was drawn after the accursed philosophy." Also the words of Rabbenu Bachya (Nos. 5 and 6 in the two groups respectively) seem to be mutually contradictory. It would seem rather unlikely that these authorities revised their opinion from one extreme to the other, so that these contradictions pose a riddle to the student.

## 2. Natural Sciences vs. Humanities

The resolution of these apparent contradictions becomes quite simple once we note that our Sages distinguished clearly between the natural sciences and the humanities. They looked upon the natural sciences as the common property of all nations, but restricted the study of humanities to divinely revealed sources and to sources derived from these. This distinction is based on the fact that, in the area of humanities, the required information was revealed to us by God (in the Torah), whereas the natural sciences were left to us to discover on our own. And thus it ought to be: in the realm of the natural sciences, our senses offer opportunities for more or less objective tests of our hypotheses, whereas in the humanities we lack all objective criteria and, when left to ourselves, must resort to arbitrary standards — groping in total darkness as we make our choices. Here the situation would be totally hopeless without divine revelation. This explains why revelation concerns itself just with this area, defining our purpose in life and our duties on earth. Anyone passing by such revelation willfully, and seeking the same information on the basis of conjecture, is wasting his efforts, negligent, and is inviting errors of the most fundamental kind. No wonder the study of non-Jewish philosophy, bearing on questions of ethics, was disparaged by our Sages.

Our Sages said:[19] "If someone tell you there is science among the [other] nations, believe him; Torah among the [other] nations, do not believe him." This is perhaps their most explicit statement of the above idea. For the term Torah is used in the Bible for moral instruction and is the closest Biblical term for our "humanities."

We find this distinction adopted even in *halakhah*:[20] "He who sees gentile sages — who are wise in worldly sciences — says: 'Blessed is He who gave of His wisdom to flesh and blood.'" — "For the wisdom of the gentiles also comes from God."[6] The authorities explain that this refers to the other sciences[21, 22] and excludes Torah and theology.[22, 23]

When we go through the two listings given in the preceding section, we find indeed that all the praise refers primarily to the natural sciences and all the expression of disapproval to the humanities.

The role of the natural sciences in Torah life was investigated elsewhere.[24] Here let us probe the *halakhah* concerning the humanities.

## 3. Specific Prohibitions

Let us now investigate more specifically the prohibitions and the definitions of the terms used in this connection.

### 3.1. THE "SCIENCE OF GREEK" (*Chokhmath Yevanith*)

The Mishnah states:[25] "During the campaign of Titus, they decreed against the diadem of the bride and that a man may not teach his son the 'science of Greek'." The Talmud adds to this:[26] "Cursed be he who teaches his son the 'science of Greek'."

Rabbi Yitzchak Bar Shesheth (RIVaSh)[27] was asked what, specifically, was meant by the "science of Greek" and whether this included Aristotle's *Physics* and *Metaphysics*. In his reply, RIVaSh refers to the above Talmudic passage, which he quotes extensively — partly as follows:

"When Jerusalem was under siege . . . there was an old man who knew 'science of Greek' and he told them in 'science of Greek'. . . at that time they said: Cursed be he who raises pigs (a pig was involved in the incident cited) and who teaches his son 'science of Greek'. . . Greek is different from 'science of Greek'." He then continues: "From this it is evident that those books are not included in that prohibition . . . Therefore it seems to me that 'science of Greek' refers to speaking Greek in riddles and in an obscure manner which the general public do not understand."

Rashi[26] explains it similarly as "an artful language spoken by courtiers, which the general public do not understand" and elsewhere[28] he explains it as "hints." Also RaMBaM,[25] Meiri,[25] and Rabbi Shim'on ben Tzemach (RaShBaTz),[29] all explain it similarly. Rabbi Loeb of Prague (MaHaRaL) wrote:[6] "It is evident (from the Talmudic passage) that 'science of Greek' refers to figurative and artful speech." (There seems to be only one among the early halakhic authorities who disagrees with this definition — Rabbi Meir Halevi (RaMaH) identifies it with astrology.[30])

In conclusion we cite an interesting passage from the *Chavoth Ya'ir*;[31] the author prefaces one of his responsa with the statement: "Love Socrates, love Plato, but love truth even more" — and then proceeds with a long list of references of Torah-authorities, all of whom quoted this statement!

### 3.2. "EXCLUDED BOOKS" (*Sefarim Chitzoniim*)

In the Mishnah[10] enumerating those who do not share in the world-to-come, R. Akiva includes also those who read "excluded books." In our version, the Talmud explains this: "The books of the Sadducees.* Rav Yosef says, it is also forbidden to read the Book of Ben Sira." Rabbi Yitzchak Alfasi's (RIF) reading is: "Books that explain the Bible arbitrarily, without relying on the interpretation of the Sages, because this approach has heretical aspects." R.E. Wasserman[32] explains the statement, that the readers of such books have no share in the world to come, as follows: "This does not refer to a transgression of a prohibition against reading; it means that he will have no share in the world to come due the the [resulting] atheism."

The Jerusalem Talmud explains: "Excluded books: for instance the Books of Ben Sira and the Books of Ben La'ana. But the books of Homer and all the books written from then onward, it is as if he read a letter... they are given for contemplation — not for toil." One authority (*Margaliyoth HaYam*[11]) expresses amazement at the fact that the Book of Ben Sira is treated more severely than those of Homer, even though Ben Sira is quoted in the Talmud several times. He suggests that the Sages prohibited only those books which were written close to the time the Bible was canonized, lest these be inadvertently included into the Scriptures. In a similar vein, it has been suggested[33] that this passage refers to books canonized by the Christians and that these were forbidden lest they be considered part of the Scripture written in the Holy Spirit.

RaShBaTz seems to interpret "excluded books" to refer to foolish books. He writes[29] that the Talmud explains this term to refer to the books of Ben Sira and Ben La'ana: "these are books full of perversions, such as physiognomy (i.e. judging personality from facial features), histories; and also heretical books which contain no wisdom and are a mere waste of time... but books based on evidence are not included in this."

### 3.3. BOOKS OF IDOLATRY AND HERESY

The reading of books of idolatry is generally forbidden. RaMBaM writes:[34]

---

* RIVaSh's version is "heretical books" and he consequently forbids those books of science whose tendency it is to uproot principles of faith as belonging to this category.

"The idolators wrote many books concerning their service ... God commanded us not to read these books at all." Also Scripture states explicitly:[35] "You shall not learn to do like the abominations of those people."

Books of heresy are those that teach atheism or the rejection of Torah. The reading of these, too, is forbidden. Indeed, heresy is more serious than idolatry. Concerning heretics and their books, Rabbi Tarphon said: "Should they come into my hands [Torah scrolls written by a heretic] I would burn them, together with God's name [written] in them. For even if a man pursue you to kill you or a snake to bite you, you may enter a house of idolatry [to save your life], but not one of their houses, for they know and rebel."[36]

The source of this prohibition is the verse:[37] "You shall not investigate after your heart" — "That refers to heresy."[38]

The verse:[39] "Remove your way far from her" is also interpreted[40] to apply to heresy, as well as the verse:[41] "All those who come to her shall not return; they will not attain the paths of life." The reason for the greater severity reserved for heresy is seen in its dangerous attractiveness.[42]

### 3.4.  LEARNING FROM A HERETIC

The Talmud states:[2] "He who learns [even] one thing from a *magus* is guilty of a capital transgression." Rashi there explains that a *magus* is a heretic who seduces to idolatry and that it is forbidden to learn from him even words of Torah. This law is included in the *Shulchan Arukh*.[43]

## 4.  Reasons for the Prohibitions

A number of reasons are cited as underlying these prohibitions. We survey these here.

### 4.1.  DANGERS TO SPIRITUAL INTEGRITY

We quoted earlier the warning of Rav Hai Gaon[15] that whosoever diverts his attention from Torah study and occupies himself with philosophy instead, will throw off, bit by bit, the yoke of Torah and reverence for God, until he leaves Torah and prayer entirely. Two later authorities[27,44] illustrate by means of examples from our history, how the study of philosophy has misled even the greatest among us. "This should make everyone conclude: If these two kings (of Torah) could not maintain their position ... how can we, who never really saw light?"[27]

The *Sepher Hayashar* writes in a similar vein:[45] "There are studies that destroy faith, such as the excluded and the heretical studies and philosophy ...

He should with all his might keep far away from all of these because he will lose his faith ere he derives any benefit from them. Unawares, bit by bit, philosophy will remove [from Torah] him who occupies himself with it . . . unless he have an expert and pious teacher who will instruct him — and protect him from those places which weaken his faith; thus a man can avoid the pitfalls of philosophy and, yet, attain the desired benefits."

### 4.2. LACK OF VALUE OF THESE STUDIES

RaShBaTz explained "excluded books" to refer to foolish books and according to him the prohibition of their study seems to be based on the law:[46] "You shall speak of [words of Torah] — and not of other things."

R. Ya'akov Emden said[47] concerning the study of logic that "it causes much waste of time." Another authority wrote concerning such study:[48] "One man comes and builds a tower reaching the sky, and bases it on conjecture. Suddenly comes another and pushes it away, the walls fall . . . and in vain have its builders toiled."

In the same spirit Rabbi A.Y. Bloch wrote:[33] "The study of literature and the reading thereof and all the popular studies that have no practical value — it is certainly not worth while to spend time on these."

### 4.3. "SESSION OF SCOFFERS" AND "INCITING THE EVIL INCLINATION"

*Sepher Tehilim*, in the opening Psalm, praises the man who "never sat in a session of scoffers." Consequently such participation is forbidden.[49]

The *Shulchan 'Arukh*,[50] based on earlier authorities,[51] decrees: "Belles-lettres, secular parables, and romances, such as the Book of Emanuel and books of wars — it is forbidden to read these on Sabbath, and even during the week it is forbidden, as a 'session of scoffers', and concerning romances there is the additional prohibition against inciting the evil inclination."

## 5. Permissible Aspects

We now list certain conditions under which it is permissible to relax the above prohibitions.

### 5.1. "SCIENCE OF GREEK"

The Talmud[52] permits those who are close to the royal court, such as the house of Rabban Gamliel, to speak in "science of Greek." Indeed, Rabban

Shimon ben Gamliel is quoted[52] as saying: "There were a thousand children in my father's house; 500 learned Torah and 500 learned 'science of Greek'." The reason for the permission is not given there.

Meiri[52] explains the permission on the ground that the kings accepted fully only people conversant in the sciences. This seems to imply that they are permitted because it is part of their profession. Another reason given for the permission is the opportunity it provides to save lives.[53]

The Talmud[53,54] also permits teaching "science* of Greek" to one's daughter, "because it is an ornament for her." This is explained[53] as enabling her to attain the good graces of influential courtesans and is thus in the category of those close to the royal court.

## 5.2. PHILOSOPHY AND EXCLUDED BOOKS

The prohibition against the study of philosophy and the excluded books is also not absolute. Such study is permitted primarily when necessary to qualify the student to "reply to the heretic."

This permission is based on the following Scriptural interpretation:[55] "You shall not learn to do" — "such study is forbidden when it is meant for doing; you may, however, study in order to understand and to give guidance." Rashi comments on this that the study is permitted when it is done for the purpose of fulfilling God's commandments.

Meiri explicitly relates this passage to the study of excluded books. He comments on the Mishnah[10] which forbids the reading of excluded books, that this prohibition applies[11] only "when the reading is not for the sake of understanding and giving guidance."

In a similar vein RaMBaM comments on the Mishnah:[29] "Know what to reply to the heretic," that "we should study material which will enable us to respond to the challenges of the heretic, and . . . even though this involves studying foreign philosophies, we must be careful not to accept any of their ideas." Here he clearly implies that for a proper cause, such study is permitted.

RaShBaTz commented on this same Mishnah: "On this basis we permitted ourselves to read the books of their errors in order to enable us to respond to them successfully, based on their own words."

---

\*   The reading there is "Greek"; but from the context it is evident that "science of Greek" is meant. There, in reference to teaching one's son, a number of authorities specifically have the reading "science of Greek".

Similarly MaHaRaL:[6] "Concerning study from their books which contain words against the Torah . . . there is a danger that the reader may be drawn after their words and arguments . . . However, if his intention is 'to know how to respond to the heretic'. . . [such study] is certainly permitted, if his intention is to know their words, so that he will be able to reply to a heretic, for this is an extremely great obligation."

Concerning logic, R. Ya'akov Emden wrote;[47] "Although one should not waste time on the study of logic . . . a little is beneficial as a preparation for the battle of the tongue, to foil the heretic's conquest. However, though a little is good to develop the mind and to further social communion, nevertheless much of it is harmful." Elsewhere[56] he wrote: "One should first study the Torah and afterwards the secular studies, in order to know how to reply to those that err and to refute their arguments."

Also Rabbi A.Y. Bloch, the late Rosh Yeshiva of Telze, wrote in his landmark responsum[33] that individuals will occasionally have to read such books to save others — and themselves — from losing their way in the paths of falsehood and also because it enables them to know how to answer the heretic.

### 5.3. LEARNING FROM A HERETIC

In his discussion[6] concerning the importance of secular studies, MaHaRaL writes: "But the matter needs further consideration, since it is forbidden to learn from an impious teacher . . . This applies [only] when he learns directly from this impious teacher and he has a personal attachment to him . . . but not to study from their written works."

R. Ya'akov Emden also refers to the problem of learning from a *magus*, in a responsum to a pupil who was studying medicine at a university far from Jewish settlements. There[47] he writes:

"It is therefore proper to study [medicine], but not to forsake, because of this, the sweet and holy study [of the Torah]. Blessed is he who takes hold of the one without forsaking the other, to follow in the footsteps of [RaMBaM, Rabbi Moshe Ben Nachman (RaMBaN) and many other great teachers of the generations gone by]. But to my mind it is not proper to go far away to their universities, even if this is not in the category of learning from a *magus*, nevertheless: do not approach the door of her [heresy's] house and do not desire to be in their rooms . . . to learn their customs and manners."

## 5.4. STUDY OF HISTORY AND LANGUAGES

In the Tosaphoth[57] we find the following ruling: "Those histories of wars written in foreign tongues, it seems to R. Yehudah that it is forbidden to read them [on Sabbath] and even on weekdays, Rabbi Yitzchak (RI) did not know who permitted reading them, since they are in the category of 'a session of scoffers.'" As already noted, these words are cited in the *Shulchan 'Arukh*.[50] *Be'er Hetev* comments on this:[58] "This does not apply to *Yosiphon* and *Sepher Hayuchsin* and the History of Rabbi Y. Hacohen, for from these one learns admonishment and reverence, and similarly from *Shevet Yehudah*."

In his *Mor Uketziah*,[50] Rabbi Y. Emden comments on this: "These matters may be perused only on weekdays. Most of it is the history of past gentile kings and there is no need to know them. Therefore it is forbidden to read them on a steady basis, except during times of relaxation, when he is exhausted from Torah study . . . in order to learn from them correct and polished style."

He then continues with several reasons justifying a small amount of study of non-Jewish history.

(1) So that the *Talmid Chakham* will not lack the basic knowledge of history and will not appear unschooled in worldly matters.

(2) Occasionally such study may throw light on Jewish history.

(3) Such study can help guide political decisions, especially when dealing with gentile governments.

Among the recently published responsa of R. Mendel Kargau* appears a letter[59] to a former student of his, who had decided to study at a university in order to satisfy the government-imposed requirements for the Rabbinate. R. Kargau warns him of the dangers lurking on his chosen path, but also analyzes the importance of secular studies. Among his remarks: "Nevertheless one should not neglect other areas of knowledge, for it is inappropriate for a man of stature to be missing any science, especially grammar . . . and similarly for other areas of knowledge that do not mislead [mathematics and languages] and Rabbi Yoseph Shlomo of Kandia called these 'secular, with the purity of the holy.' In general, any knowledge we acquire will nurture us with pleasure, besides the fact that, eventually, the benefit will surely

---

* Author of the definitive work *Giduley Taharah*, lived in XIX century Germany at a time when the Reform movement tried to harness the force of the German government to an effort to uproot Orthodoxy.

come. And the Rabbis who lived before us, even though they were very great in Torah, would have done better had they acquired some of the [secular] knowledge instead of attempting to reconcile strange *Midrashim* with false interpretations. Had they done so, the forces of destruction [Reform] would not have come upon us, the forces who destroy every good element."

The *Ba'al Chazon Ish*, too, wrote[60] that "history is highly instructive to the wise; he will base his wisdom on the developments of the past."

Concerning the study of foreign languages, we find that it was customary already in the period of the Gaonim (1000 C.E.) to teach these in school:[61] "In the name of Rav Hai Gaon we are told that one may teach children of the synagogue Arab script and arithmetic, together with their Torah study — but separate from Torah study, it is not appropriate."

In his program of study for "one who wishes to be a wise man in Israel," Rabbi M. C. Luzatto recommends[62] that he study, after *completing* the study of Bible with its major commentaries, the Talmud, RaMBaM's Code, *Shulchan Arukh*, and *Midrashim*, also composition, including prose and poetry.

Rabbi Yechezkel Landau (author of *Noda BiYehudah*), in opposing any program of study which would undermine the supremacy of the Torah, nevertheless stresses the importance of learning the language of the country. He said:[63]

> "Nevertheless, the praise of manners and to know the language of the gentiles precisely, I, too, laud these greatly . . . and we find that in the Bible, also, we were taken to task for not knowing foreign languages . . . He who has foresight will grasp both; he will take Torah as primary, but learn also polished language and good customs."

Similarly, his son and successor to the Rabbinate of Prague, wrote,[64] that, "together with the study of Torah, the children should learn the German language thoroughly, together with other subjects. This is very important . . . It is obligatory on each father to teach his son the language and customs of the country in which he lives."

The study of the language of the host country seemed to be customary throughout the ages and all over Europe. This is also evident from many of the published regulations of Talmud Torah schools [e.g. those of Cracow (1595)[65a]; Verona (1688)[65b]; Venice (1714)[65c]; Altona (1805)[65d]].

When Rabbi Samson Raphael Hirsch prepared the program for his high school[66] (perhaps the first attempt at a modern Torah-based high school), he included a good deal of secular subjects as auxiliary to Torah study and as part of the duty to train one's son for a livelihood. In this respect he simply followed the lead of our great authorities throughout the ages. It is interesting to note that he included history and language (composition), but not literature, despite its possible great ethical content that he was well aware of.[67] All this in perfect agreement with the opinion of the earlier authorities. In the words of Rabbi A.Y. Bloch:[33] "Why search for gold among refuse and mud, when we can gather pearls from a place of purity."

Also Rabbi Simchah Zissel Ziv, one of the greatest leaders of the Mussar movement, introduced the study of language, arithmetic, and geography into the program of his Talmud Torah schools (both in Kelm and Grubin), motivating them as auxiliary to Torah.[68]

## 6. Summary

To summarize our findings: Although the Sages praised the study of the natural sciences (as auxiliary, though subordinate to Torah study), they opposed, as a rule, the study of humanities and philosophy from non-Torah sources. Such study is often dangerous to the spiritual integrity of the student, without offering much potential benefit. It is permitted — possibly even important — only in certain exceptional circumstances.

The value of the study of history depends on the subject matter, the teacher, and his intent. Portions of history may actually fall into the category of Torah and others are a total waste of time and fall into the category of "a session of scoffers." Others are not part of Torah study, but are appropriate for the spiritual leader to acquaint himself with them.

Basic secular subjects, such as the language of the land and arithmetic, seem to have been always an integral part of the schooling of the Jewish child.

## 7. Epilogue

In conclusion, I would like to add a few remarks, evaluating the problem in view of the special conditions prevalent today.

Our situation differs from pre-emancipation conditions in that a major portion of our people has become estranged from their Torah heritage — and this fact has specific *halakhic* implications.[69] The *'arevuth*-principle,[70] which makes every Jew responsible for every other, obligates us to draw close even those who have fallen prey to total heresy,[71] and this, in turn, requires us to have a common language with them: "I doubt that anyone today knows how to admonish (effectively)."[72] Since in today's culture, concepts of history and literature have become key elements of the language of the man-in-the-street, the duty to develop a common language would seem to call for some familiarity with history and literature.

If such studies are indeed called for, we may be able to minimize the accompanying loss of Torah study by investing them with Torah values. With careful planning, it should be possible to use the study of world history to demonstrate the working of divine guidance ruling the nations and to use gentile philosophy and selections from their literature, dealing with basic human problems, to contrast the Torah approach with that of the secularist. This might even be a powerful tool for clarifying the ideology of the Torah in the language of the student and enable him to gain deeper understanding thereof.

True, the development of such a program is a major undertaking requiring profound Torah knowledge and understanding. But those devoting themselves to this noble task may themselves reap unexpected insights as a due reward for their dedication.

## REFERENCES

1. Baraitha, *Responsa of RaMBaM*, Mekitzey Nirdamim, Jerusalem (5718), No. 150.
2. B.* Shabbath 72a; Isaiah 5, 12.
3. MT* Yesodei HaTorah 4, 12.
4. *Chovoth Halevavoth*, S. Habechinah 2.
5. R. Bachya to Avoth 3, end.
6. MaHaRaL, *Nethivoth 'Olam*, Nethiv Torah 14.
7. R. Ya'akov ben R. David Proventzali, "Responsum on Science Study", in *Divrei Chakhamim*, edited by R. E. Ashkenazi, p. 71.
8. R. Eliyahu, Gaon of Vilna, cited in the introduction to Euclid, translated into Hebrew by R. Barukh of Sklow.
9. R. Mosheh Sofer (*Chatham Sofer*), *Sermons*, p. 112 (P. Beshalach).
10. B. Sanhedrin 90a.
11. B. Sanhedrin 100b.
12. B. Sotah 49b.
13. B. Berakhot 28b as interpreted by *Menorath Hamaor*, Para. 267. Note that Rashi *loc. cit.* interprets the statement differently.
14. Sifra to Leviticus 18, 4.
15. R. Hai Gaon, cited in Letter of RaMBaN "Terem A'aneh" (ed. of R. Chavel, p. 350).
16. R. Bachya to Deut. 30, 12.
17. R. Hai Gaon in poem "Mussar Haskel".
18. Yoreh De'ah 179, 13. The word "the accursed" is missing in the Vilna edition. Cf. B. Landau, *Hagaon Hachasid MiVilna*, Ch. 17, note 10.
19. *Midrash Rabba*, *Eichah*, 2, 13.
20. *Shulchan 'Arukh*, Orach Chayim, 224, 7. Based on B. Berakhot 58a.
21. *Sepher Mitzvoth Katan*, Para. 148.
22. *Levush*, Orach Chayim, 224, 7.
23. *Beth Yosef*, loc. cit.
24. L. Levi, "Science in Torah Life" in *Challenge*, A. Carmell & C. Domb, eds., Assoc. Orth. Jew. Sci., London/Jerusalem (5736), pp. 94–110. A more extensive version in Hebrew appeared in *Yad Re'em*, Jerusalem (5735), pp. 189–216.
25. Sotah 9, 14; according to R. O. Bartinura's version. Cf. also the note of R. Akiva Eiger there.
26. B. Sotah 49b.
27. RIVaSh, Responsa, No. 45.
28. B. Minachoth 64b.
29. Avoth 2, 14 (*Magen Avoth*, there).
30. *Shitta Mekubetzeth*, B. Bava Kama 83a.
31. Responsa *Chavoth Ya'ir*, No. 9.
32. *Kovetz Shey'urim* II, No. 47.
33. *Proc. A.O.J.S.* 1, 106–112 (5726) & *Hama'ayan* $16^3$, 11–16 (5736).

*B. — Babylonian Talmud; J. — Jerusalem Talmud
MT. — Mishneh Torah — *Yad HaChazakah* of RaMBaM

34. MT, *'Avodah Zarah* 2, 2.
35. MT, Teshuvah 3, 7.
36. B. Shabbath 116a.
37. Num. 15, 39.
38. B. Berakhoth 12b.
39. Prov. 2, 19.
40. B. 'Avodah Zarah 17a.
41. Prov. 2, 19.
42. B. 'Avodah Zarah 27b.
43. Yoreh De'ah 179, 19.
44. R. Yosef Ya'avetz, *Or Hachayim* Ch. 8.
45. *Sepher Hayashar* 6, s.v. *Midah 'Asirith*.
46. Deut. 6, 7; B. Yoma 19b.
47. *Sheilath Ya'avetz* I, No. 41, end.
48. *'Oleloth Ephrayim*, Introd., s.v. *halo tov*.
49. B. Kiddushin 41a, B. 'Avodah Zara 18b, Avoth 3, 2.
50. Orach Chayim 307, 16.
51. R. Asher (ROSh) to B. Shabbath Ch. 23, 1, end.
52. B. Bava Kama 83a.
53. J.* Shabbath 6, 1, Korban Ha'eidah.
54. J. Peyah 1, 1.
55. Deut. 18, 9 & Sifrey there. See B. Shabbath 75a for list of citations in B.
56. *Siddur Beth Ya'akov*, "Hanhag. Talmud Torah" 2. Cf. also Pirkei Avoth 2, 14 in this *Siddur*.
57. B. Shabbath 116b, Tosaphot, s.v. *vekhol sheken*.
58. Orach Chayim 307, 18.
59. Responsa *Giduley Taharah*, No. 7, in A. Sofer, *He'aroth VeHearoth . . .*, Kedem, Jerusalem (5736).
60. *Emunah Ubitachon* 1, 8.
61. *She'erith HaNachalah*, p. 13, R. Y. M. Chazan, editor.
62. *Derekh Chokhmah*, end.
63. *Derushey HaTzelach*, No. 39.
64. Introd. to *Doresh Tzion*.
65. S. Assaf, *Mekoroth LeToldoth HaChinukh BeYisrael*, Tel Aviv (5714), a.I., p. 101, b. II, p. 155; c. II, p. 191; d. I, p. 267.
66. *Horev*, Ch. 84.
67. Cf. his "Schiller-Rede", Ges. Schriften Vol. 6, pp. 308–321.
68. D. Katz, *Tenu'ath HaMussar* II, p. 183.
69. Cf. *Melamed Leho'il*, Orach Chayim 29 and *Chazon Ish.*, Y.D. 2, 16 (end).
70. B. Shavu'oth 39a (end).
71. E.g. MT Mamrim 3.3 and Chafetz Chayim letter, cited in R. Y. D. Epstein, *Mitzvoth Hashalom*, p. 295.
72. B. 'Arakhin 16b.

# PROCEEDINGS OF THE AOJS
# VOLUME 1

## CONTENTS

169

# PROCEEDINGS OF THE AOJS
# VOLUME 2

CONTENTS

# PROCEEDINGS OF THE AOJS
# VOLUME 3-4

## CONTENTS

# Addresses of Contributors
# to this Volume

Rabbi Dr. Immanuel Jakobovits
Office of the Chief Rabbi, Adler House, Tavistock Square
London W.C. 1H 9HN
England

Professor Yaakov Choueka
Dept. of Mathematics & Computer Science
Bar Ilan University, Ramat Gan, Israel

Rabbi Menachem Slae
Institute for Informational Retrieval & Computational Linguistics
Bar Ilan University, Ramat Gan, Israel

Dr. Samuel W. Spero
Cuyahoga Community College, Metropolitan Campus
2900 Community College Avenue
Cleveland, Ohio 44115

Rabbi Dr. Reuven P. Bulka
JOURNAL OF PSYCHOLOGY AND JUDAISM
Center for the Study of Psychology and Judaism
1747 Featherston Drive
Ottawa, Ontario, Canada K 1H 6P4

Professor Hugo Mandelbaum
Givath Beth Hakerem 1/37
Jerusalem, Israel

Dr. Moshe HaLevi Spero
1669 MacIntyre Drive
Northwood 4, Apt. =1669
Ann Arbor, Mich. 48109

Rabbi Aaron Levine
575 Grand Street
New York, N.Y. 10002

Professor Leo Levi
46 Bayit Vegan Street
Jerusalem, Israel